GOD Schooling

GOD
Schooling

How God Intended Children to Learn

THE GUIDE *for* HOMESCHOOL PARENTS

Julie Polanco

NASHVILLE

NEW YORK • LONDON • MELBOURNE • VANCOUVER

GOD Schooling
How God Intended Children to Learn
THE GUIDE *for* HOMESCHOOL PARENTS

Published in New York, New York, by Morgan James Publishing. Morgan James is a trademark of Morgan James, LLC. www.MorganJamesPublishing.com

The Morgan James Speakers Group can bring authors to your live event. For more information or to book an event visit The Morgan James Speakers Group at www.TheMorganJamesSpeakersGroup.com.

ISBN 978-1-68350-863-2 paperback
ISBN 978-1-68350-864-9 eBook
Library of Congress Control Number: 2017918185

Cover Design by:
Rachel Lopez
www.r2cdesign.com

Interior Design by:
Bonnie Bushman
The Whole Caboodle Graphic Design

In an effort to support local communities, raise awareness and funds, Morgan James Publishing donates a percentage of all book sales for the life of each book to Habitat for Humanity Peninsula and Greater Williamsburg.

Get involved today! Visit
www.MorganJamesBuilds.com

To Ed—
who tolerated eating sandwiches and
soup for dinner while I finished this book.
I love you, and thank you.

Table of Contents

Acknowledgements

I thank Jesus Christ, first of all, for giving me the material for this book and for saving me from my sins. I thank Justin for being patient with my frequent calls and incessant questions and David for being approachable. I thank my design and marketing team for embracing my vision. Thank you to the worship team at Emmanuel Bible Church who cheered me on and encouraged me through the publication process. And, I thank my family for tolerating me through the long journey that brought this book to fruition. I couldn't have done this without all the beautiful people that God put in my life.

How to Use This Book

If you read my first book, *Finding Joy*, then you will be happy to know that I have kept most of the original text and added some more personal stories. You will note that I have added a chapter on teenagers and left more space for your own reflections and Bible study related to this book. I encourage you to ask the Lord to speak to you directly about issues raised in your heart and about quoted Bible passages.

If you have not read my first book, then get ready for a whirlwind adventure through secular and Christian thought on child development, education methods, what God says in his Word about it, and my own adventure and insight as we go. There are study questions at the end of each chapter to help you dig deeper into what you have learned. This book can even be used as a study for a group of moms wishing to explore natural learning together.

The names of my children have been changed to protect the innocent. In this book, my oldest daughter is Tiger; my oldest son, Hawk; my younger daughter, Butterfly; and my little boy, Mouse.

All Bible verses quoted in this book are from the New International Version (NIV) unless otherwise noted.

PART 1

Dispelling Myths

Chapter 1

Biblical Support for Natural Learning

W hen I first decided to homeschool my kids, I had no idea what it would be like, but I was sure it was going to be great. I had visions of obedient, respectful children who were so excited to learn, they hung on to my every word and couldn't wait for the next new topic. I poured over curriculum catalogs and magazines, my mind whirring with all the possibilities. Everything looked so attractive and promised hours of learning adventures. Everyone promised that their product would create a love of learning in my children, that it would be easy to do, that my children would be successful, and on and on.

I have to admit that I am a sucker for glamorous advertising. I loved books and nifty paper crafts so much, I wanted to believe that what they said was true. Maybe you have done this, too. I chose activities based on what I thought would be fun, what I enjoyed doing, and if I liked it, surely, the kids would like it. Right? Oh, sure. I read some books on learning styles, and I even read some books on different methods of homeschooling. There were elements of Charlotte Mason that I liked, and there were elements of classical education that I liked. I thought that unit study was a great idea, too. The only method that I definitely stayed away from was textbooks.

In spite of all my enthusiasm, things were not all rosy and wonderful. By the time my oldest daughter, Tiger, was seven years old, I was beginning to burn out already. I had been in the habit of spending hours poring over catalogs and websites trying to find the perfect books and activities. I spent my free time writing up objectives, lessons, questions, crafts, and more. I invested so much of myself in trying to come up with the perfect teaching materials, but when I would try to present everything I had so painstakingly prepared, I was faced with…

Moans and groans. Hawk and Tiger talking at the same time and laughing while I was reading. Stick figures and sloppy coloring instead of neat work (Tiger's drawings that she did on her own were amazing, but she never put in that kind of effort for me). Slumping in the chairs, laying on the table, making noises with their mouths, their feet, their hands. I would go to the bathroom and when I would come back, they would have disappeared. Can you relate?

When Butterfly was born, I felt I could no longer do this and needed a curriculum. Well, that was not the answer, either. In the next year, Hawk refused to do any lessons I asked him to do. I am not saying that he didn't learn anything; he just didn't want to learn anything from me. I took it personally. Who did he think he was trying to exert some control over his own learning? I saw him as a disobedient little boy, and I am ashamed to say that he spent far too many days looking at the wall. I had tried bribery with candy and other treats, but he didn't care. He didn't care about looking at the wall, either. At first, I thought that was what I needed to do. A child must learn obedience, right? Except that my discipline wasn't working. He was detaching from me and acting out in other ways.

He was not the only one who exhibited problems. My daughter, Tiger, talked to me about her dreams less and less and was bordering on depression, and the baby, Butterfly, was challenging. I hadn't even been parenting that long, I hadn't even been homeschooling that long, and everything seemed to be unraveling. *God, didn't you call us to homeschool? Didn't you make it abundantly clear? If we're supposed to homeschool, then why isn't it working? I thought that doing Your Will would give me joy. I don't have any joy. I want to give up, and if you don't do something, I'm putting them in school next year.* He answered my cry, but not in the way I expected. I had hoped that He would make my children more obedient to my plan. Instead, He led me on a journey to make me more obedient to *His* plan.

He led me on a journey to re-examine my goals, my relationships, everything. It has not always been an easy journey, but God is a patient and loving teacher. He made sure that I learned what I needed to learn (and continue to learn still). Where he led me was to a life without school, what many would call an unschooled life. The things that he taught me along the way, the things I discovered through prayer and experience, are recorded for you here. Join me on my journey where I finally found joy and peace.

Enslavement Versus Freedom

One of my favorite verses from the Bible regarding natural learning, or what some call unschooling, is Galatians 5:1: "It is for freedom that Christ has set us free. Stand firm, then, and do not let yourselves be burdened again by a yoke of slavery." Paul was writing regarding the legalistic religious requirements of his day. We are not only free from religiosity but anything that can *become* religious or dogmatic.

Curriculum can be a great tool as long as it does not become our religion. What do I mean by that? Anything that we follow just for the sake of following it, anything that we become so dedicated to that we feel like a failure if we don't follow its dictates, anything that enslaves us with its rules, can become our religion. Curriculum is meant to be a guide to help us accomplish our goals. The curriculum is not the goal. Too many times I have heard moms say something like, "Well, Michael is still in third grade this summer because we didn't finish the curriculum." Whoa! The curriculum has usurped the family's goals or become the family's goals. These moms have become slaves to their chosen curriculum; it has become their religion.

In my own journey, as I said, I started out creating my own unit studies but, when my third child, Butterfly, was born, I felt I needed a curriculum. All the time I was using this curriculum, neat ideas for things to do with my three small children kept floating into my head. *Hey, remember that article you saw about the egg floating on the water? That would be really fun to try. Hey, there's a neat website about dead logs. You should check it out and take them out to the woods. Today would be a great day to visit the arboretum. Weren't you going to make a cave diorama with little bats and stuff?*

As fun as they sounded, I sadly ignored them, rationalizing that I was distracted and that I needed to finish the curriculum first. I condensed it a bit, but I was determined that because I had spent $300 on it, I was going to finish it. Even though it was not appropriate for my four-year-old, Hawk, even though my seven-year-old, Tiger, was getting tired of it and only put in a half-hearted effort, I was going to stick with it and finish. I had allowed it to take control of my home, and it had become a religion to me. However, I did not learn my lesson at first. I bought the curriculum several times over the course of the years, but used it for shorter and shorter periods of time. It was like the devil was putting doubts in my ear, whispering, "Gee, it's going to be hard to get to the library every two weeks or so. Maybe you should get a curriculum and save yourself the trouble. Yeah, it's a few hundred dollars, but what's your time worth? You could use it again or sell it later. Come on. It looks so fun."

I became enslaved to the fears that drove my decision. Maybe you have some of these fears. I was afraid that my child wouldn't measure up next to her public-schooled peers. I feared the close scrutiny of relatives. I feared that she might have gaps. I feared I wasn't challenging her enough and that I wasn't doing enough. If she didn't understand something that was commonly taught to her peers, then I worried that there was something wrong with her or that I was doing something wrong. I wanted so badly to do everything right and I was so afraid that I was doing everything wrong. It was such an incredible burden that it finally sank me into depression. It was then that God gave me a vision of what it *could* be like.

Be Still and Know I am Lord

He began to speak to me about homeschooling and the first thing He said was, "Be still and know that I am Lord." Does my story sound like your story? Are you in that place where you are desperately searching for a different way? Do you feel restless and uneasy, burdened by worries and fears? Be still. *Know* that He is Lord. Know that *He* is Lord. Know that He is *Lord*. Do you really truly believe that God is Lord of your life or do you say it with head knowledge, not heart knowledge? Do you truly know that you are *not* the lord of your life? Do you truly understand what being lord means? These words spoke directly to my heart because I have struggled with control in my life. God spoke truth into my circumstances.

Because all my life I had always felt like everything I did was for someone else's approval and someone else's agenda, I was desperately trying to gain control of something and that something ended up being my children. In all my life, I felt that I had never done anything just because I wanted to. Even the choice to homeschool was for the benefit of the children, at first. I had to give up the dream of graduate school and endure the pain of ostracism because now I was just a housewife. I had to admit to God that I was resentful and controlling. He began to show me all the blessings of being at home, that He loves me, that all that has happened in my life has been turned to good, and that I need to fully surrender to Him to be able to fully receive His joy. And, as often happens when we abandon ourselves to Him, he gave me back my dreams. He enabled me to take freelance writing projects and to write this book. Now, I am writing more books under my own name and as a ghostwriter.

It took several weeks of meditating on what it means to be still and know God to begin to fully comprehend what He was saying to me. When it started to sink in, my burden began to feel lighter. Joy and peace slowly started to seep into my heart. He began to lead me toward becoming more relaxed in my homeschooling approach. He put in my heart a desire to serve other Christian women who felt led in the same way. Suddenly, I had companions in my journey that I didn't have before. He began to direct me to websites and blogs about a lifestyle of learning, relaxed homeschooling, and Christ-led unschooling. As I relaxed, he showed me, through the children themselves, how He leads them to discover his truths.

May 14, 2007

Today, I just let them play outside all day. It was hot, and I just felt like giving them a break. They came up with plenty of their own learning experiences, though. Tiger made several attempts to figure out how to make a bucket of water tied to a string dump its load into a bowl waiting below, for instance.

They pretended to be cells and put stickers on themselves to represent DNA.

July 2, 2007

The kids got up late. In fact, I had to wake Tiger up. That was fine, though, because she stayed up late asking me questions about God and the why of it all. We went to Fullersburg Woods with another homeschool family, and we were there for 2 hours doing the longest trail they have. They saw butterflies, frogs, a heron, fish, cicadas, other insects, and of course, many trees and plants. They poked around in the water, climbed trees, looked into likely animal homes, and other stuff kids do in the wild.

Many of us start homeschooling in a spirit of fear, as I was describing earlier. We are afraid that the school environment will harm our child, we are afraid that the schools aren't doing enough for our child, we are afraid that our child won't have an edge when it comes to college, and on and on.

Jesus said, "Come to me all you who are weary and burdened and I will give you rest. Take my yoke upon you and learn from me, for I am gentle and humble in heart, and you will find rest for your souls. For my yoke is easy and my burden is light." (Matthew 11: 28-30). His yoke is to simply follow him. That is what He told all of His disciples: "Follow me." There are no other requirements. But when we follow Him, He says, "Love the Lord your God with all your heart, all your soul, and all your mind." (Matthew 22: 37). These two verses taken together mean that I can come before Him, lay down my worries and my fears, sit at His feet with complete and utter devotion, and simply obey.

Simply obey. What does that mean? When Jesus was at the home of Mary and Martha in Luke 10:41-42, Martha was distracted by all the preparations, and she got angry because her sister, Mary, wasn't helping her. Instead, she was sitting at the feet of Jesus. Jesus basically said that Martha worried too much and should sit at his feet, too. Obeying means that we keep our eyes on Him, not on the distractions of this world, not on all the preparations that we supposedly need to be doing. If we are walking closely with the Lord, He will show us exactly what to do at exactly the right time.

An example that comes to mind is something that happened recently in Tiger's life. Tiger is now eighteen and, in her last year of high school, she took a class at the junior college near us. I had been thinking that she ought to take general education classes there so that they would transfer to a university if she later chose to go. God had a different plan. As I was driving home from the city thinking about how she should register soon, He clearly said to me that she should take a class that would teach her how to use software. *Software?* I thought. *How weird. That won't transfer, but okay, God.* When I got home, I looked through the course catalog and pointed out to Tiger courses that taught software. One of them was called Digital Art. She thought that sounded interesting and it would introduce her to the Adobe Creative Suite. After taking that class, she decided to take the next one in the sequence because she loved it so much. In fact, she has decided that she wants to be a graphic designer. What if I hadn't listened to God and did what I thought, instead?

Walking with God is freeing. In II Corinthians 3:17, Paul says, "Now the Lord is the Spirit and where the Spirit of the Lord is, there is freedom." It is for *freedom* that Christ has set us free. He didn't set us free to do whatever we want. He set us free so that we would be unencumbered by our past; by the mistakes of our parents, teachers, and community; and by our current hang-ups, fears, and sinful nature so that we could follow Him and become like Him. He set us free from all that would keep us from discovering and doing His Will, and that includes setting us free from the world's standards of what education looks like.

"God was with Him"

The first question every homeschooler asks me when we first meet is, "What curriculum do you use?" That is often the same question we ask ourselves when we are planning a homeschool year. What we need to ask ourselves first is, what is God's Will for this child? And, a corollary to that, what is God's Will for my family? We say we trust God, but then we plan out each and every moment of our children's lives right up to college, sometimes even picking the college. Do we truly, truly trust God? Do we truly believe it when Paul writes in Ephesians 2:10, "For we are God's workmanship, created in Christ Jesus to do good works, *which God prepared in advance for us to do.*" Or, do we say to ourselves, "Well, yes, but we don't know what God has planned so we better make sure our son is prepared for anything." If God has prepared these works for your child to do, then won't He make sure that s/he is adequately prepared for them? Doesn't He prepare you to do His Will in the most miraculous, mind-boggling ways that have very little to do with your own efforts? Do you think that the Creator of the Universe would leave your child's future, His future, entirely in your hands? Remember, our children are being prepared for a future that doesn't exist yet. That includes more than just careers.

My son, Hawk, spent many of his early years building stuff. He built with Legos, mostly, but also with wood, clay, and later, with metal. Over time, he developed the unique capacity to know how to make almost anything from whatever materials were at hand. I thought for sure this would mean that he would grow up to be a carpenter or maybe even an engineer. Then, two things happened in 2016. He had the opportunity to learn how to use the machines in a fabrication lab, better known as a

Maker Lab, and he wanted to learn how to do 3-D animation out of a love for Pixar and DreamWorks films.

He was hooked. He was particularly interested in 3-D printing his own creations and soon learned how to do 3-D modeling as well. There has suddenly been a watershed of opportunities for him in this field, leading him to gain the attention of game developers. In addition, he won second place in an entrepreneur competition, earning him enough money to buy a 3-D printer for himself. God just opened door after door for him in ways I could never have imagined, let alone planned. His early years prepared him to have an understanding of 3-D objects that would never have come if he hadn't been allowed to spend his time "playing."

There are many examples of this in the Bible as well. Let's look at the lives of two famous figures from the Old Testament and how God provided for their futures. First, let's look at Joseph. How did he gain favor with Potiphar? Was it with his vast knowledge? Was it with his charm? Genesis 39:2-4 says: "The Lord was with Joseph and he prospered and he lived in the house of his Egyptian master. *When his master saw that the Lord was with him* and that the Lord gave him success in everything he did, Joseph found favor in his eyes and became his attendant." It was Joseph's character, his righteousness before God, that brought the success, not Joseph himself. In fact, it was the physical body of Joseph that brought him to prison. So, it was not Joseph's stellar academic training that brought him success. How did he rise to become the right-hand man to the king of Egypt? He was in prison. It was God who reminded Pharaoh about Joseph, and it was God who gave him the dream interpretation that led to his high position. Joseph would have died in prison if it were up to his own efforts.

What about Daniel? He was royalty, so surely his academic training brought him success. In Daniel 1: 3-5, the Bible says, "The king ordered Ashpenaz, chief of his court officials, to bring in some of the Israelites from the royal family and the nobility—young men without any physical defect, handsome, showing aptitude for every kind of learning, well informed, quick to understand, and qualified to serve in the king's palace. He was to teach them the language and literature of the Babylonians. They were to be trained for three years and after that, they were to enter the king's service." Verse 17 says, "To these four young men, *God gave knowledge and understanding of all kinds* of literature and learning. And Daniel could understand visions and dreams of all kinds." God gave it. Their previous learning meant little to the Babylonians, only that they had the aptitude. Again, it was God who raised Daniel to a position in the government through the dream interpretations that He gave Daniel. Remember, the king was going to have all the magi killed because no one could tell him the meaning of his dreams. Daniel would have died with the other magi if his success were based on his own efforts.

In both Joseph's and Daniel's story, God used their character to bring glory to himself in a pagan country and to save his people from destruction. His plan wasn't dependent on what they did or what their parents did. There was no possible way that these great men could've studied enough to prepare themselves for God's plan. Only God could prepare them for God's plan. The one thing we can do, and are admonished to do, is to do what their parents did—train our children in righteousness, "Love the Lord your God with all your heart and with all your soul and with all your strength. These commandments that I give you today are to be upon your hearts. Impress them upon your children" (Deut. 6: 5-7a). We are to use the Bible to do it: "All Scripture is God-breathed and is useful for teaching, rebuking, correcting, and training in righteousness, so that the *man of God may be thoroughly equipped for every good work.*" (II Timothy 3:16).

Do not Despise, Hinder, or Offend

In Ephesians 6:4, we read, "Fathers, do not exasperate (meaning irritate, annoy, excite the anger of) your children; instead, bring them up in the training and instruction of the Lord." We must train them according to God's ways, not our ways. We are to train them using biblical teaching, not worldly teaching. I don't think that we are talking about just spiritual matters, but also about the way we treat our children when we are teaching them the academics, too. If we are admonished not to exasperate our children, then why do we ask them to do things that they are not developmentally able to do? Why do we punish them for following their God-given passions because they aren't obeying us in doing what the world says they should be doing? Are we exciting the anger of our children, causing them to seem disobedient, by our unbiblical teaching methods? We should examine our relationships with our children and ourselves to see if this is so. We need to guard our relationships against losing our children to the enemy because of our zealous attitudes about academics.

Jesus says, "If anyone causes one of these little ones who believe in me to sin, it would be better for him to have a large millstone hung around his neck and to be drowned in the depths of the sea." (Matthew 18:6). The King James version uses the words "offend one of these little ones." Ouch. How can we cause our little ones to sin? One of the major ways that we do this is by overlooking character issues in favor of academics. If we are so busy teaching a curriculum, driving around from activity to activity, or just plain overloading the day with too much schoolwork, when do we have time to address poor character development? If we do not deal with a child's moral behavior, it is the same as teaching them it is okay. Another way we do this is through our examples of pride, self-righteousness, and idolizing. If we are overly concerned with academics and fall into these sinful behaviors, are we passing these sins on to our children?

In Matthew 10:14, Jesus told the disciples to "let the little children come to me and do not hinder them, for the kingdom of God belongs to such as these." Many of us homeschool so that our children will receive a Christian education, but sometimes our methods actually hinder our children from developing a true and lasting relationship with Jesus. As I mentioned earlier, my controlling behavior with my children harmed our relationship and gave them a false idea of what it means to follow Christ. A touch of legalism crept into my homeschooling and parenting style. Following Jesus is freeing, not rule-based. It wasn't until I applied the principles of God's grace and leading to my interactions with them that real Christianity broke through.

Another attitude we need to guard against is thinking that children are insignificant, not worthy of respect, lower than adults, or are not as important. That includes thinking that their opinions don't matter. Jesus said, "See that you do not despise one of these little ones. For I tell you that their angels in heaven always see the face of my Father in heaven." (Matthew 18:10) Our children have definite ideas about what they would like to know, how they would like to learn about it, when they are ready to do it, and where they want to be. When my son says, "I want to watch a Ken Burns documentary tonight downstairs on the couch while I'm eating chips," do I answer him with, "Well, I bought you a history curriculum and you haven't touched it. In fact, you give me a hard time about it every day. No, you cannot watch that"? If I do, I am despising him as a child of God who is worthy and valuable. We need to treat our children with the same respect as we treat adults. Their opinions and thoughts matter just as much as ours and, by listening to them, we may be encouraging them to listen to the voice of the Holy Spirit stirring within them.

If we put biblical character training and knowledge of and passion for Jesus at the center of our lives, God will add all the other training to it in his own timing, not our timing. Jesus says in Matthew 6:33, "But seek first His Kingdom and His righteousness, and all these things (food, clothing, etc.) will be given to you as well." Proverbs 3:5 says, "Trust in the Lord with all your heart and lean not on your own understanding; in all your ways acknowledge him and he will make your paths straight."

Hollow and Deceptive Philosophy

I know what you're thinking. Those skeptical little voices are there in the back of your head saying, "What about reading, writing, and calculating? I mean, I know God has a plan for each child's life, but he does expect competency in these areas, doesn't he? You can't do anything without these skills." Yes, these are essential skills for life. No, God would not want your child to grow up without these skills. However, does a child really need to know how to read at age five? Who decided that all ten-year-olds should know their multiplication tables? Colossians 2:8 warns, "See to it that no one takes you captive through hollow and deceptive philosophy, which depends on human tradition and the basic principles of this world rather than on Christ." Now, Paul was referring to rules and restrictions regarding diet, worship, and other practices, but I would argue that it could also apply to *any* unbiblical philosophy dependent on human tradition that causes us to trust more in the world or our own deeds rather than in Christ.

Many people believe that it is a good idea to start teaching children when they are as young as three years old. Preschool is practically required these days, and if a child doesn't go, well-meaning folks shake their heads as though the child will be an adult delinquent. Historically, until the late 1970s, society pitied families who put their young children in preschool because it meant that the husband didn't make enough money for mom to stay home. How times have changed. I am no different, even though I worked at two different preschools while in college and saw first-hand what that environment was like.

I saw that my oldest was a bright little girl, and from about age four until we did curriculum, I did unit studies with her that I designed. I was so excited about homeschooling that I couldn't wait to get started.

We did units on the American West, fish, Abraham Lincoln, and more. But, even though I had thought I had planned interesting topics, she always seemed resistant. I thought this was an obedience issue. The truth was that I was misguided in thinking that I had to formalize her learning, that I had to "do lessons" with a four-year-old. God taught me the hard way that the world's practice of teaching little children formalized lessons is unnecessary and can even be harmful. Let me tell you what I mean.

David Elkind writes in his book, *Miseducation: Preschoolers at Risk*, "educational programs intended for school-aged children are being appropriated for the education of young children." He claims there is no research that shows that teaching academics to preschoolers is beneficial. The voices in my head asked, "What about the research that says..." I discovered that many supposed research claims were promoting a product, such as early reading or early foreign language DVDs. Anxiety and stress disorders are rising among children under the age of six because of the stress of trying to please parents and teachers who demand that they do things that their young brains were never intended to do.

Before I had begun my teaching agenda, Tiger would be interested in something with great passion. First, she was passionate about dinosaurs and wanted books about dinosaurs, dinosaur movies, dinosaur figures, you name it. Then, she saw *Lion King* and became passionate about big cats. Then, she saw *Mulan* and suddenly wanted to learn all about China. This was probably the Holy Spirit working in her, igniting passions that would stay with her for the duration of her childhood. But, like many well-meaning parents, I took these interests and made them into unit studies (as I was describing above) for which I began requiring certain tasks. I would ask her to copy words or short sentences. I would ask for her to regurgitate what I had read to her. I would ask her to do matching activities or other cut-and-paste-type lessons. Many of these activities are popular with parents, but boring to children. Because

I was unfortunately following scope and sequence charts at that time, the requirements were based on those charts, not on what my child wanted to do. I believe that this is the reason she stopped sharing her passions with me after a while. She also lost some of her adventurous spirit and became avoidant of anything that carried the risk of failure. Unfortunately, this persisted for a long time. Thankfully, God rescued her from me when he began speaking to me about becoming more relaxed. You see, He loves her too much to let me ruin her. He loves your children too much to let you ruin your children, too. Don't buy the popular notions that children should learn to read by age five or that formal foreign language study should begin when they are toddlers or any number of other myths. It is all deceptive philosophy that changes like the wind and disregards the child's true needs. We will explore this in more detail in the second half of this book.

Christian Versus Secular

We can also be deceived by our own inaccurate perceptions and biases. Unschooling has been perceived, in Christian circles, as a situation in which the parents have a very hands-off attitude about parenting and education. The stereotypical family would be one in which the children did no chores, played all day (sometimes playing video games all day), and told the parents what they would and would not do. The parents in this scenario sit and read their own books and interact with their children only when the children wish it. In my own experience, this is a highly skewed stereotype of the radical unschooler. I am not promoting this extreme interpretation, but more of a natural learning approach that captures the original ideology of this term.

Unschooling was a term coined by the late John Holt, who was the first educator to support homeschooling. It was first used in 1977 in *Growing Without Schooling*, the nation's first magazine dedicated to homeschooling (also started by John Holt). He invented this term to describe learning that is interest-driven, child-led, natural, organic, eclectic, or self-directed, according to Pat Farenga in the updated version of *Teach Your Own: The John Holt Book of Homeschooling*. Holt also used the term to make the distinction between homeschooling, an often parent-led endeavor, and unschooling or natural learning, a more child-led endeavor.

I have come to believe that the heart of unschooling is freedom within parental limits. This means freedom to choose what to learn about, but as a Christian, there are certain topics that we would not immerse ourselves in, such as witchcraft or homosexuality, except to perhaps better understand our own faith. This means freedom to choose what to do, but as a parent, I have set limits such as one hour of screen time, with few exceptions, and that my children must do chores. Unschooling means allowing your children to choose what they would like to learn about and when and how they would like to do so. It means helping them to achieve their goals by working with them to organize their time. It means respecting their individual developmental time table. And, because they do not know all the possibilities, it is our job to expose them to all the richness and beauty of the world and let them sample its delights. I recognize and collaborate with God and what He is doing in each child's life rather than acting as though their futures are all up to me. Unschooling can be a very deliberate endeavor, not necessarily haphazard.

Some people like to criticize unschooling by saying that it is unbiblical. Are the public school and its methods more biblical? Is reproducing the public-school methods in the home more biblical than what I have described above? Those who fully embrace the possibilities that unschooling can offer are poised to *suck the marrow out of life*, to live a richer and more meaningful life. It casts off grade levels, grades, tests, scope and sequence, records, scores, and all the other trappings of school that we have been brainwashed into believing are necessary.

God did not create schools; He created families. Jesus Christ did not teach His disciples by doing what the Romans did; He taught them through His relationship with them and using stories and experiences that would capture their hearts. Children are not fifth graders or first graders or sophomores; they are eleven-year-olds, six-year-olds, and sixteen-year-olds. We do not need to study ancient Egypt this year just because curriculum XYZ says so or because the other kids of the same age are doing so.

Let's cast off all this nonsense and just live life together more fully. Let's read together, play games together, make things together, sell things together, go places together, talk and laugh together, explore together, and build our relationships with each other. God told us to teach and train our children. We can do that within the context of life. We can guide, lead, teach, train, reproach our children and be deliberate about their moral character and preparation for God's calling on their lives without being school teachers (in the figurative sense). All of that is more effective within the context of a loving and respectful relationship. Children are more receptive to our instruction if we have their hearts.

Study Questions

1. How are you feeling right now? Evaluate whether your education choices are contributing to your feelings.

2. Who or what is the lord of your life?

3. What does freedom mean to you? Are there things that keep you from enjoying that freedom and why?

4. How can you trust God more with your children's futures?

5. Does the idea of unschooling scare you? Why or why not?

6. What do you feel is God's Will for your child, for your family?

Chapter 2

Motivation & Excellence

Wen my son, Hawk, was twelve years old, he was learning Tae Kwon Do. At first, I would come in with him. After only two classes, he said to me, "I don't think I want to keep going, mom. It's too hard." I didn't say anything at first. Part of me felt what he felt, especially since I saw how he struggled and how the teacher drilled them. The other part of me spoke up and ultimately won the tug of war in my heart.

"Hawk, I will bring you early so you can get extra practice, but I am not going to let you quit." Why didn't I let him quit? I knew that he had the ability to succeed if he applied himself and that if I let him quit at this, he would learn how to be a quitter, never doing anything that required hard work. I wasn't going to make that mistake again, although with Tiger there was more to it.

Tiger had been involved in local gymnastics for a few years and had developed ability, especially on the bars. She had made it to the pre-team level, but the girls were caddy. There was one girl in particular who was trying to force Tiger to kiss her and be her girlfriend. Tiger had been exposed to things that we didn't approve of as a result of this girl trying to befriend our daughter. We later discovered that this girl had tried to trap our little girl in her house alone with her. In order to cut off this "friendship," we had to remove Tiger from gymnastics. Tiger had also expressed that she was afraid of failing and disappointing others as well as herself. On a deeper level, she was afraid that her best wouldn't be good enough. At the time, I wished that there was another gymnastics program nearby that she could participate in, but I was also a little glad. Gymnastics is expensive and, unfortunately, we had to commit to the entire year at a time. We didn't want to pay out another thousand dollars for our daughter to participate half-heartedly. We could use the money for something else. Did we think she was lazy? Not at all. She worked very hard. Do I think that she learned that it was okay be a quitter, that maybe we thought she was right to quit? Perhaps. Would you allow your daughter to be manipulated and molested by a lesbian so she could be a great gymnast and learn to never quit? I know you wouldn't, and we weren't willing to do that, either. She still struggles with motivation and challenge, but I know that God is working on her.

External Motivation

What is motivation and how does it work? What motivates you to do well? There are two main ways to motivate a person. One is through external motivators, such as grades, awards, or a raise in pay. The other way is by tapping into a person's internal motivation. External motivators are things done *to* a person to get him to comply with our wishes. Internal, or intrinsic, motivation comes from within the person and stems from his/her own desire to succeed and do well. We will first discuss external motivation, and from now on, we will be talking primarily about children.

In the book *The Motivation Breakthrough* by Richard Lavoie, creator of the best-selling PBS video series *F.A.T. City*, he argues that there are eight basic motivational forces that inspire human beings to act and put in sustained effort. He claims that each person has a unique combination of these motivators that makes up his/her individual motivational profile. He organized these eight motivational styles into six types of teaching strategies to address those styles. He issues several warnings in his book about the effective use of these motivating strategies, which I will not go into here.

Some of these motivational forces can be in direct conflict with biblical character traits. Traits such as the need to be important, the need for prizes, or the need for recognition might be better examined in light of whether that child understands his worth and the worth of others in the sight of God. And, as Alfie Kohn, psychologist and author of twelve books as well as an ardent critic of modern education, writes in his book *Punished by Rewards*, some of these can actually undermine motivation in the long run. For example, a child may have a motivational profile that includes the need to belong. If a strategy of people-and-praise isn't handled correctly, the child may end up shackled to people-pleasing instead of being empowered. Understanding your child's personality type in this area can be very helpful if it's handled correctly and can even enhance intrinsic motivation.

Butterfly is motivated by having a sense of ownership over projects, but she likes to work with others. She kept hounding me to find a way for her to get together with her friends because she wanted to do a play. I never really got around to talking with their parents, but she wanted to do it so much that she took the initiative and called them herself. She coordinated practice times. She helped write the script and create the props. She made the playbills and signs. It was amazing to see how industrious she was. The final production was impressive and a fabulous demonstration of what four motivated girls could do on their own.

However, most of the time, we as parents don't get it right. We want our kids to do what we want so badly that we are willing to bribe, coerce, and punish in order to get our children to do what we want. That is not in the spirit of how God would have us treat our children. In Ecclesiastes 7:7, we read, "Surely oppression and extortion make a wise man foolish, and a bribe destroys the understanding and judgement" (Amplified Bible), and Proverbs 15:27 says, "A greedy man brings trouble to his family, but he who hates bribes will live." Other verses that allude to the sin of bribery include I Samuel 8:3 and I Samuel 12:3. I believe that God not only frowns on us when accepting bribes from others, but that he frowns on us when offering bribes as well. Isn't offering some sort of external prize to motivate a child to do what we want a form of bribery and doesn't it teach our children how to bribe others? Giving prizes for reading a certain number of books, giving money for memorizing Bible verses, or giving candy for completing worksheets are all forms of bribery that we would do well to avoid. It only teaches our children how to manipulate people, which is really a form of bullying.

There are many critics of external motivation, and those who advocate for natural learning generally try not to use external means of motivating children. John Holt, educator and author of ten books, says in his book *Learning All the Time,*

> "the trouble with any kind of external motivation, whether it be negative (threats or punishments) or positive (grades or gold stars), is that it displaces or submerges internal motivation. Babies do not learn in order to please us, but because it's their instinct and nature to want to find out about the world. If we praise them for everything they do, after awhile they are going to start learning, doing things, just to please us, and the

next step is that they are going to become worried about not pleasing us."

Charlotte Mason said much the same thing in her series of books on education. Children who do things just to please adults possess a weakened character. What if that adult isn't around? Have you ever witnessed the phenomenon of a child being naughty as soon as his parent is out of the room? If you have, then you understand what I mean. Children who only do right because they are afraid of being punished will often do wrong when there is no threat of punishment. It is the same with education.

The fact that a child is born with internal motivation is evident in every toddler who is allowed to explore under the watchful, loving eyes of his mother. Most young children are impatient to try new things, to stretch themselves to see how high they can fly. What happens after age five that children begin to lose interest in trying hard, to be satisfied with minimal effort, to believe that life isn't worth chasing anymore? When children go to school, they are no longer encouraged to be whatever they want to be. They are no longer allowed to explore at will. They are no longer allowed to fail and laugh about it. Suddenly, their dreams are stolen from them. They are made to sit still and do what someone else wants them to do all day, and failure is something to be avoided at all costs. Is it biblical to replicate this system in our homes?

When children are coerced into doing academic tasks instead of encouraged to explore, say, creative writing (or any other topic), as they become interested, Kohn reports that they are less likely to become *naturally* interested in those very topics. Being rewarded for doing creative writing is not likely to result in a love for creative writing, but quite the opposite is true. Kohn states that "rewards smother people's enthusiasm for activities they might otherwise enjoy... Extrinsic motivators are most dangerous when offered for something we want children to *want* to do." I saw this in action when teaching Hawk to read. The more I forced him to practice reading, the more I made him do reading lessons, and the less desire he had to read on his own. In fact, he announced that he hated reading and did not pick up a book for a long time. I will talk more about him later in the book. I also saw this with a popular kids' Bible study program. I picked up Tiger and a few of her friends from this program and I asked them, "Would you learn all these Bible verses and be in such a rush to finish the books if there were no prizes?" The car grew quiet and one of the girls said, "No." In contrast, Butterfly chose to participate in another Bible study program that has parallel tracks for children and adults, but there are no prizes. The prize is simply knowing and understanding God's Word. Butterfly continues to participate year after year and loves it.

Why does coercion of any kind have such a negative impact on motivation? Maybe kids think that it must not be fun or interesting if we are offering something else in addition to the learning experience. Maybe children feel that we lack confidence in their ability to see the importance of something, to be able to figure things out on their own. In this way, we inadvertently scorn them and they feel it, even if they can't express it. They may say things like, "It's boring" or "It's hard" or "Why do I need to know this?" If you listen between the lines, you'll hear the cry of their hearts.

Now, you're probably saying to yourself, "How many kids are going to just jump up and down to learn their times tables? There are some things that a child just has to learn." I agree—there are things that a child just has to learn. But, we can coerce our children with prizes and punishments for doing or not doing their math worksheets and guarantee that they will hate math. Or, we can gently invite them into our lives and show its importance and relevance to our everyday experience. Activities such as shopping, paying bills, planning parties, cooking, building projects, sewing, and more might just trigger the question, "How do you do that?" and maybe, just maybe, they will be willing to learn their times tables to make life easier for themselves.

I know. You're probably saying to yourself, "Yeah, right. I have taken my kids shopping, and they may ask about sale prices and count out the money to pay for a candy bar, but they are definitely not jumping up and down to learn about long division or anything else about math for that matter." After my children learned their math facts, I often only did informal math for several years before high school. Hawk was very stubborn about not doing things that weren't relevant to him. If he couldn't see the reason, he wouldn't do it. Math was one of those things. I was so afraid my son would be math illiterate. Well, when he was fifteen-and-half-years-old, it became relevant for him to learn algebra. He did the entire textbook in about 4 months. More importantly, he excelled at it. He excelled so much, I thought he was cheating and contrived ways to prove that he was. All I ended up doing was proving myself wrong. Don't worry so much. God's got it all under control.

That brings me to the other reason rewards smother people's intrinsic motivation. Rewards are experienced as controlling, and people like to retain control over their own destinies. The extent to which the environment is controlling through rewards/punishments, threats, surveillance, evaluation, deadlines, being ordered around, or by competition is the extent to which a person will lose their intrinsic motivation.

I have seen examples of this in observing children on class field trips. What I generally observe is children carrying a packet of worksheets and running from exhibit to exhibit to fill in the answers on their worksheets. I have never seen a group of children stop for more than 2 minutes at any exhibit, and most of the discussion amongst the children is of the "this is gross/stupid/silly/weird" variety. The only way children truly learn anything at museums is if a caring adult takes the time to go through it with them, which I do see occasionally. However, what might have otherwise been quite interesting to them has been reduced to blanks on a worksheet, an obstacle to overcome in order to get the grade/praise/goody from the teacher. Think about your own school experience. What was the best thing about field trips? A day out of school!

Another example of this happens in Sunday school programs at the church. The Bible is God's love letter to us. It is worth reading in order to know God better and to know how to live for Him. Think about the example I gave above. Why do we need to give prizes for memorizing Bible verses? Are we inadvertently telling kids that they wouldn't want to read the Bible unless they were getting a prize for it? I wonder how many children stop reading their Bibles when the prizes and games end.

How do we avoid this? How do we motivate kids without giving grades, prizes, candy, or money to get them to do schoolwork? How can we escape a legacy of standing over our children, threatening to withhold privileges, giving extra chores, or sending them to bed early if they do not complete their schoolwork? There are several answers, but no strategy works on its own. A person has to want to be his best, choose to be his best, because that's what he wants for himself. He is internally motivated toward excellence, because he enjoys the satisfaction and pride that he feels within himself when he knows he has done a great job for the Lord, as mentioned in Galatians 6:4: "Each one should test his own actions. Then he can take pride in himself, without comparing himself to somebody else." I know, your burning question remains: how do we encourage a child to want to do his best without threats and without jeopardizing our relationship with him? How do we tap into his natural internal motivation? In what situations do we want him to do his best?

Using Intrinsic Motivation

While we do not want to extinguish that inner spark that motivates every little child, we recognize that sometimes a child needs a bit of guidance, encouragement, and focus. Even in a home that encourages natural learning, we would be remiss and not very tuned into our children if we did not offer this help when needed. Mary Hood, a homeschooling pioneer and author of three homeschooling books, mentions three ways to tap a child's intrinsic motivation in her book, *The Relaxed Home School*. The first happens when a person is internally motivated to learn something, the second occurs when someone else has an intense love of a subject and transfers their enthusiasm to the student, and the third form of motivation comes when people set goals that have personal significance to them and are willing to do things that are difficult or boring in order to reach them.

The first type of motivation occurs when children want to know something, want to explore something, because that "thing" sparks their interest. This is the type of interest that Tiger showed after she saw *Milan*. Mouse has shown this type of enduring interest in rodents. Somewhere, he saw mice and was so fascinated with how cute they were that he decided that he needed to carry around a mouse puppet with him everywhere. Then, he wanted to look up all kinds of facts about mice, rats, and other small creatures, using the internet. He draws mice warriors and makes up stories about them in his mind, including their weapons, their houses, their armor, their enemies, their jewels (that's another of his interests), and their history. That is intrinsic motivation. At one point, I was writing a short "reader" every day featuring mice so that he would want to read the adventure. (Was I using some form of bribery there? Hmmm.) His interest in mice grew to encompass storytelling, drawing, sewing, sculpture, engineering, and science without me having to do anything but accompany him on his journey. It has been very sweet.

The second type can perhaps best be summed up by two of the principles outlined by Oliver DeMille, founder of George Wythe College and author, in his book *A Thomas Jefferson Education*. Inspire, don't require. Mentor, don't teach. We need to be engaged in exciting learning projects and opportunities ourselves. We need to take our children to new places and sometimes even make changes in our lifestyles so that we can be more engaged with our communities and larger world. Jesus taught his disciples and inspired them through His example. Our children learn more from our example than from any textbook or lecture that we might give them. Are our lives worth emulating? Are we conveying the right messages about what is important and valuable? If our example is to spend hours on the computer, then that is what they will learn to do. If we spend time visiting with the elderly, writing letters to free political prisoners, or crocheting blankets for new single mothers, then that is what our children will find important and valuable.

How do you spend your time? Do you have a home business? Do you spend a lot of time on social media? Do you spend your days driving your kids from one class to another? Are you active in a co-op? Do you have hopes and dreams that you have put on hold while your children are small? I know that all of those things have been true of me at one time or another. One thing that I have been intentional about, though, is trying to embrace my dreams now and bring my children along for the ride. They are watching me, and I want my daughters to know that being home doesn't mean that they have to sacrifice themselves on the altar of motherhood. I want my sons to see a real woman, not a person who is there for their needs only. But, in other ways, I am not always consistent. I get distracted. I wake up late. I talk too long on the phone. I go on errands in the middle of the day. I get caught up in a great book and lose track of time. I schedule too many appointments in the same week. Dear sister, don't beat yourself up when you do these things. Every day is new! We all just need to be aware of our habits and whether or not it is what we want our children to emulate. We want to motivate them through our lives.

I heard Nathan Levy, an Illinois teacher specializing in gifted kids, discuss the third type of internal motivation that Mary Hood mentioned, the type where children choose their goals and are willing to do whatever it takes to reach them. This includes pushing through failure and difficulty. He said a child needs to be in situations in which it is possible for him to fail. He needs to feel uncomfortable, stretched, frustrated because true success, true self-confidence, comes from getting up one more time than you fall down. He needs to know that excellence is the goal, not perfection. He needs to learn to persevere. Levy added that children need to learn how to perform under stress. If kids don't learn that, then anyone can knock them down by making them nervous. Of course, they need lots of practice in order to be equipped to perform. In order for this to be an effective way to motivate and teach a child, the child has to choose the situations and understand what he needs to do to reach his goals.

Learning to play an instrument is an excellent example of this. When Butterfly and Hawk were learning to play violin and guitar, respectively, there were times when they had to play for an audience and their teachers weren't there. It was painful for me to watch their eyes scan the crowd, not finding the person who was supposed to accompany them. I saw the fear and disappointment casting shadows across their faces and waited to see if they would still have the courage to play. Each of them did. They may have made a couple of mistakes, it may not have sounded as full as it would have, but each of my children played anyway and learned valuable lessons about themselves.

I have also seen this principle at work on playgrounds. Studies show that helicopter parenting, or overprotectiveness, actually makes kids more fearful and anxious, not less. Parents who do not let their children fail at anything, even at basic things like falling off the monkey bars, set their children up for a lifetime of being afraid under stress. I have even heard of a play place for kids that prohibits parents from being on the playground because there are actually more accidents when the parents are present. How about that! Let them fall down, and they will learn to pick themselves back up, avoiding anxiety about failure. Anxious kids will have too much self-doubt to push past the hard knocks of life to reach their goals.

Other ways to teach perseverance can include exposing children to folks who are master craftsmen. Children (and adults, too) often think that something is easy until they actually watch something being done from start to finish. My children visited a violin maker and got a chance to see firsthand how these beautiful instruments are made. They went backstage at an opera house and learned that the wigs are strung by hand with human hair. Hawk and Tiger got an opportunity to try blacksmithing and see just how long it takes and how hard it is to craft tools from iron. These are just a few of the adventures we have had to help all of them learn what hard work and perseverance can accomplish.

Kohn offers some other suggestions for tapping intrinsic motivation. He says that, first, we need to foster a sense of discovery by allowing time for active learning, not just seat work; discuss the reasons for the work you are requesting them to do (as I have shared above in reference to math); ask open-ended questions to draw out their curiosity; welcome mistakes; and, as already stated before, set an example. Work *with* your children, give them meaningful things to learn about, and allow them to make choices about their learning activities. This is what natural learning is all about!

Using Chores to Teach

One area of life where the demands of the task teach the child motivation and excellence is in the area of work. I don't know too many people who enjoy cleaning the cat litter box, taking out the trash, or shoveling snow. But, we can all see the immediate necessity of doing these things. There is no mysterious "someday you will need to know this"; instead, there is a very real consequence now if you do not do the work.

Because we want our children to love learning, we should never use study as a punishment or disciplinary tool. In its place, chores and manual labor can be assigned or encouraged for a number of reasons:

1. To teach diligence and excellence, as a job well done is easily measured and the pain of having to redo a poor job is memorable.
2. To teach self-worth and self-confidence. A child who feels he is contributing to the family in a tangible way feels his importance as others depend on him.
3. To teach competence in life skills. The child will one day need to care for his own family and home.
4. To teach the child to serve and care for the needs of others. By learning to help, he will see the joy he brings to others and learn true happiness.
5. To help the child learn about himself and his abilities. An independent child is confident and knows himself.

There is a great book, *Life Skills for Kids* by Christine M. Field, which lists appropriate chores for each age group, starting with age two. This *is* possible. My youngest daughter, Butterfly, at age four was responsible for feeding our two cats and the fish. She was expected to make her bed, water the plants, and dust low shelves and tables as well. Because of her age, I had to remind her and work beside her of course, but she understood that she had important work to do for our family and was happy to do it.

Recently, I left for a writer's conference in the middle of the week. Hawk, Butterfly, and Mouse were left home all day for 2 days, with my husband returning from work in the evenings, of course. My mother asked me, "Who's with the kids? How are they going to eat?" I said, "Mom, Hawk is sixteen and Butterfly is nearly thirteen. They can take care of themselves, and they all know how to do everything. They don't need me there." It felt strange to say that, but they all know how to cook and clean, even Mouse. That is the goal, isn't it?

Service and entrepreneurship done as a family can also be powerful ways to teach a child about the importance of excellence. If he is shoveling a widow's steps and sidewalk, she could slip and fall if he doesn't do a good job getting all the snow off the pavement. If he is making a product for sale, no one will buy shoddy work.

All of these ideas bring us back to intrinsic motivation. It is very tempting to use gold stars to get kids to do their chores. What if you just left that pile of dirty dishes on the counter, waiting for that child to wash them or load them in the dishwasher? Will you have enough clean dishes to serve dinner? What if you left that tub dirty, just waiting for your son to scrub it? Will he enjoy taking a bath in a scummy tub?

I do not tie chores to an allowance, although I know many families that do. I want my kids to help out because they understand that they are an important member of the family, not because they will get something for it. What they do get is the satisfaction of knowing that I need them, that I appreciate them, and that I believe that they are capable. They, in turn, help me because they genuinely care about me and see it as an expression of their love.

What About Excellence
This brings us to the question of excellence. Much of society measures excellence by letter grades and test scores, including many homeschoolers. Families who embrace natural learning do not measure excellence in those ways. While it is true that children do not always know what they are capable of if they are not challenged to study harder, these families realize a letter grade has no intrinsic meaning outside of the boundaries of a school, unlike other ways of measuring excellence. Grades are artificial measures of effort, and because they are artificial, they don't really measure anything. Do they give a true measure of how well a child

can reason, how well a child can apply his knowledge to new situations, or how much a child has actually integrated into his understanding of the world?

I know what you're thinking. How could I say that grades don't measure anything? The child who works hard and puts in the best effort gets the *A*, right? Well, not necessarily. Let us suppose that the straight *C* student is also putting in her best effort and may even stay after school regularly to receive special tutoring, but still the highest grade she ever gets is a *C*. Teachers and college admissions officers assume that, because of this child's grades, she cannot handle college level work and is not accepted to universities. The truth, however, reveals a different story about this girl. Firstly, she has had poor instructors in key subject areas, and secondly, she is a late bloomer whose brain didn't mature enough to handle abstract learning until she was eighteen, not the assumed thirteen. At eighteen, she is actually a brilliant student.

Another scenario is the straight *A* student who never has to exert any effort whatsoever to attain high marks. What happens to this child when she faces a real challenge for the first time and has no experience in what it means to struggle and persevere because she doesn't know what her best truly is? In both cases, the artificial grading system has harmed the student and not revealed a true measure of her ability.

Natural learners know that anyone who can memorize a reasonable amount of information for a short time can get a fair grade. Children often figure out what they need to do in order to get the goodie and only do that much. I did that when I was in school. No one caught me until I didn't get the grade I thought I should in a college English class. I approached the professor about it, complaining. "Hey, I did the same work as Dawn and she got an *A*. Why didn't I get an *A*?" The professor looked at me with a smile and said, "You got a *B* because you are capable of more." Annoyed that I would have to work harder to get the same grade, I made sure I never had that professor again. What I didn't understand was that the professor tried to help me, but judging excellence with grades doesn't help anyone.

A child can have real experiences in competitions and contests that show her that it matters whether she does her best, but these opportunities are few and do not reward each individual's best effort; they only reward the best effort out of an entire group. Kohn argues that the contest mentality may actually promote the idea that other people are an obstacle to the child's success rather than possible collaborators. The contests may not bring out the best performance in a child after all, only what is necessary to win, yet another instance of doing what it takes to get the goodie. I have seen this phenomenon in my children when we used to participate in the library's summer reading program. Since each child got points for the number of books read, and not for the number of pages read, each child chose the easiest and shortest possible books in order to rack up points for prizes. That is not excellence. Needless to say, I stopped participating in these programs.

So, what is excellence if it is not a good grade, winning an award, or being the best in a competition? True excellence can be attained through intrinsically motivated activities. True excellence can be determined by how well your work stands up to a specific set of guidelines, as in professional standards of excellence, whereby everyone who attains the standard is rewarded, not just the top few. In this way, it is demonstrated by mastery of a particular area of study or discipline. True excellence is also choosing to do your best because you want to see how high you can fly. I got to see this in action for the past 2 years when Butterfly participated in a regional homeschool science fair.

First, she chose to participate in the fair. I did not make it a requirement for our homeschool. She thought it would be fun and put a lot of effort into the poster. Her project was an experiment testing compost versus regular soil for growing plants. She read all the guidelines on their website and followed everything they said without much help from me. All I did was drive her to the store for supplies, give her some pointers about her experiment, and correct her spelling. She really did the best she could, and she ended up winning a prize for her age level! The second year, she also won a prize, but it was for the most original project overall. Her project was about the sounds of the sun and planets. She did the best she could, particularly on the posters, 2 years in a row, and for 2 years in a row, she was recognized for her efforts.

Her experience brings everything together—the power of intrinsic motivation brought out by both her own passion and the demands of the task and, true excellence. Let's see what our kids can do when we believe that they can fly with their own wings, not ours.

Study Questions

1. What changes do you need to make to motivate your children without coercion?

2. How can you inspire your children?

3. How can you make your life worth emulating if it isn't already?

4. How can you improve your relationship with your children if it isn't what you had hoped for?

How Do I Get My Kids Motivated to Learn Something?

1. Do *not* offer rewards, punishments, or opinions to get compliance.
2. Offer specific encouragement, *not* generalized praise.
3. ("I like how you used several colors to make the flowers. They look lifelike," *not* "You are the best artist I've ever met!")
4. Inspire, don't require.
5. Cultivate relevant, real experiences for you and your family. Do stuff!
6. Help children set goals toward tasks of *their* choosing.
7. Allow active learning.
8. Let kids make a mess. Let them explore; get them outside.
9. Talk about reasons/relevance for your requests.
10. Ask open-ended questions.
11. "I wonder why it does that?"
12. Expose them to tasks where the requirements of the task teach concentration, effort, time, and skill.
13. Handicrafts, gardening, carpentry, instruments, etc. teach these skills well.
14. Make frequent library trips and encourage interest in anything, even non-traditional topics.
15. Pray for wisdom about your child's learning.

PART 2
Practice

Chapter 3

Thoughts on Teaching
Children Under Age Eight

When I was in college, I worked in two different preschool settings. One was a chain and seemed to me to be a regular sort of early childhood experience. The second one was inside the college, for professors and students, and had larger classrooms, trained teachers, and a better learning environment overall. What interested me about these preschools was that, in both environments, the same phenomena occurred. All the children vied for the attention of the adults. Some children were favored over others, and some children were dubbed "bad" and treated differently. All the children had to take a nap whether they were tired or not, causing trouble for the teachers. At bathroom breaks, sometimes teachers had to help kids clean themselves. Can you imagine?

The learning activities were contrived and silly. Each week had a theme, and then everything revolved around the theme. Let's say the theme was apples. The kids heard a story about apple-picking. They colored pictures of apples and talked about things that are red. The kids recited words that started with the "ae" sound. Is that really how children learn about apples? Even though I disagreed with this teaching method, I still used it on Tiger, as I shared in the last section, to my shame.

I never taught my children colors, shapes, and sizes. With Tiger, I sometimes sat with her and completed shape puzzles or took turns pushing the blocks through the correctly shaped hole to fill a ball with a colorful variety of three-dimensional (3-D) shapes. With Hawk, Butterfly, and Mouse, there were too many other things to do, but lo and behold, all of them still learned colors, shapes, and sizes. They also figured out what an apple is and went apple-picking for real.

Hawk composed his first song sitting in his high chair. He held his sippy cup in the air, rocking back and forth, singing, "My juice, my juice, I love my juice." In my ignorance, I saw this as a sign of his destiny as a great musician. I signed him up for a structured, children's music program, dragging my other two children with me (Mouse hadn't been born yet). He learned how to play two instruments. Did he remember any of it a year later when I stopped taking him? No. Did that early instruction help him learn guitar several years later? No. I did not enroll either of his two younger siblings.

With both Tiger and Hawk, I enrolled in a couple of Mommy & Me classes. I thought it might be fun to meet some other moms, do a structured activity led by someone smarter than me, and have an excuse to get out of the house. The possibility of homeschooling was still in the distance. Once there, I felt differently. Smacking a tambourine only when told to, sitting in a circle with moms who all seemed to know each other already, and chasing my children who obviously knew better than I did how dumb the whole thing was, proved to me that the classes were a waste of my time. They wanted to try all the other cool toys and instruments in the room. Who wouldn't? Why was I more worried about what the leader and the other moms thought than about my children's curiosity?

By the time Butterfly and Mouse came along, homeschooling was underway, and I stayed home. Butterfly never let me leave without her and even chased the car down the street, crying, if I did. Mouse wasn't much different. In fact, he hated leaving the house. Anytime I put him in the car, he unbuckled his seatbelt. Then, he wreaked havoc, kicking the back of my seat, throwing things at me, and pulling my hair. Later, we discovered that Butterfly has Asperger's and Mouse has many Asperger's traits, too, plus sensory issues. Riding in the car brought sensations that he struggled to manage, including the emotional waterfall that overflowed when he had to disengage from a favorite activity. He could not use words to express his frustration with any sudden changes, so he bit people, in addition to the drama in the car. Later, he took out his frustration on the objects in his room, taking every single toy and individual building block off his shelves. I spent hours reassembling his room.

Many children under the age of eight struggle with days stuffed full of planned activities and very little down time. Many more don't adjust well to being separated from their mothers for hours on end. As an employee at those two preschools, I saw that the ones who adjusted well were the children who got a lot of attention from the teachers or other children. Most of the children just resigned themselves to being there. After a certain age, they knew there was no point in crying because mom left anyway.

People criticized me because I kept my little ones with me, from breastfeeding to wearing my babies and even to a family bed until they were a year or two old. They clucked their tongues when I said they weren't going to preschool, that I knew what happened there and could do all that myself, thank you. People shook their heads and told me that my children would be clingy, that children need to learn to be independent as early as possible. They were wrong.

When my children proved to be risk-takers and bold, independent thinkers as they grew older, some of these same people said things to them like, "Hey, get off of there! You're going to break your neck!" or "You can't do that. Stop that!" or "Where's your mother? Does she know you're doing that?" Indeed, I did, and cheered them on.

In fact, children who are pushed toward independence at these young ages are often the ones who become whiny and clingy, begging for attention. These are the children who ask me to push them at the playground, me, a stranger. They ask me to watch them build a sand castle and cheer them on when they go really high on the swings. Where are their parents? Why are these children so desperate for attention that they have to get it from strangers? When I ask the children "Where are your parents?", they inevitably point to people standing far away staring at their phones, talking on their phones, or deep in discussion with other adults. The children's sagging shoulders and forlorn faces show it all. These parents have forgotten that children are a treasure from the Lord. Psalm 127:3 says, "Children are a heritage from the Lord, offspring a reward from Him."

Because children under the age of eight are often sent to preschools, they often develop trust issues. Have you ever encountered a child who says to her mother, "Well, my teacher said…"? The child believes and trusts what she learns from school more than what her parents say. This phenomenon follows the child all the way through high school. When parents do not answer their children's cries, when parents leave their little children with strangers for a good part of the day, how can little ones know for certain that their parents will always be there for them? This uncertainty and difficulty with trust causes a great deal of anxiety.

Add to that the anxiety, the stress, of being asked to do things that are unnatural for a little child. In fact, there has been a steady rise in anxiety and depression among children, even children as young as six-years-old, as I shared earlier. The new normal was considered pathological 50 years ago. Some professionals feel that the cause of this is a lack of free time to just go out and play, a lack of personal control over one's life (we will discuss this issue in greater detail in Chapter 5). However, many parents feel that play is a waste of precious time that should be spent getting ahead academically. If there really is an advantage to attending preschool, then we should see higher literacy rates, improved test scores, and higher graduation rates among high school students. Let's see if this is true.

According to the National Center for Education Statistics (NCES), 87 percent of all five-year-olds, 67 percent of all four-year-olds, and nearly 40 percent of all three-year-olds were enrolled in a preprimary program in 2015, although the program might not be full day. The Child Trends Data Bank, which compiled information from the US Census Bureau, shows that children up to age four were cared for all day by center-based programs 23 to 26 percent of the time from 1985 to 2011. With the increased use of formal preschool programs that supposedly give students an advantage, we would expect an increase in graduation rates. Unfortunately, that is not so. Over the past 30 years, the percentage of sixteen- and seventeen-year-olds enrolled in high school has fluctuated by only 2 percent, and in the last 10 years, not at all. The dropout rate has continued to hover at 5 to 7 percent. Does early reading result in higher literacy rates? No. In the last 10 years, the percentage of adults with below-basic literacy remained at 14 percent, and those with the highest levels of literacy also remained stable at 13percent. In fact, that 13 percent is low compared to the American colonial rate of 20 percent. Yes, 20 percent of the population at that time could read and comprehend such texts as Thomas Paine's *Common Sense*. Whereas, only 13 percent of the current population can do the same. Perhaps, early childhood programs give some small advantage to underprivileged groups, but overall, statistics show no advantage. If all that early schooling doesn't really give our children any advantage, then what good is it? Is it so that we can brag about how our two-year-old knows his letters? Is it so we can get a break from our children? Is it to avoid ridicule from neighbors and friends? We should question any practice that tries to justify causing children harm for the benefit of others, including ourselves. This brings me to what children of this age really need.

Think about what it would be like to land on another planet inhabited by beings that did not speak your language. Everyone dressed funny and did things that you didn't understand. Their houses, transportation, food production and preparation, culture, habits, everything—you have to learn all this in order to function on that planet. What if some well-meaning creature took you to a building and decided to teach you their alphabet before you had finished learning all you could about how this planet works? Wouldn't you be frustrated? That is exactly what happens when we put little children in classrooms. Your child must expend huge amounts of energy to make sense of a world of objects, sights, sounds, colors, shapes, relationships of size and space, animals, plants, and much, much, more. Your child really is a sponge. He *must* be a little sponge in order to just survive and understand his immediate world.

One of the most important things that a child must learn during this stage is proper behavior. As we teach them, we make the first step toward fulfilling what Jesus meant when he said, "If anyone causes one of these little ones who believe in me to sin, it would be better for him to have a large millstone hung around his neck and to be drowned in the depths of the sea." (Matthew 18:6).

An Emphasis on Virtue

In Deuteronomy 6:4-7, it says, "Hear, O Israel: The Lord our God, the Lord is one. Love the Lord your God with all your heart and with all your soul and with all your strength. These commandments that I give you today are to be upon your hearts. Impress them on your children. Talk about them when you sit at home and when you walk along the road, when you lie down and when you get up." We are to make sure our children know right from wrong in their relationship with God and with others. That is difficult to do if they are not with us. They don't learn it from sitting in a chair, listening to a teacher tell a story about a child who stole candy. They learn it from how we respond to their daily actions and how we demonstrate proper behavior through our example. We must not offend our children by allowing them to think that what is wrong is right, that what is true is false. An attentive parent can catch almost every offense and provide correction immediately.

A teacher and an aide with a room of twenty children cannot possibly catch all the offenses committed between the children. Without a Christian worldview, they may be guilty of perpetrating offenses against the children themselves. Other immature children of the same age are obviously a poor choice for teaching character. I have witnessed children behave one way when they are at school and a different way at home. They have learned two different sets of values and apply them according to the situation. At school, they have learned that to be accepted, they must go along with excluding specific kids and treating them badly. They also learn to tell lies about other children in order to gain favor. At home, they are sweet as pie, generous, and helpful. Then the parents are surprised when the teacher calls, telling them that their little girl pushed another girl into a mud puddle and laughed about it. Why the dichotomy? The child isn't learning right from wrong. She is learning to do whatever it takes to gain approval from those who will give her attention.

We should be more concerned with character development than with early academic achievement. This is absolutely vital. The basic character of a child is set by age seven, but academics can be learned at nearly any age, as we will see later.

Two notable educators write the same thing in their books. In *A Thomas Jefferson Education,* DeMille writes about the education of children in terms of three phases. The first phase, the Core phase, refers to the ages we are discussing now—children under age eight. He says that,

> "During this phase, attention should be given above all to the nurture of a happy, interactive, confident child through the lessons that occur naturally during work and play in the family setting. This consists of the lessons of good/bad, right/wrong, true/false, and is accomplished through work/play. The acquisition of 'scholarly' skills is not as important as these lessons during this phase."

Charlotte Mason emphasizes what the Bible teaches as she writes in *Toward a Philosophy of Education,*

> "In order to guarantee proper submission to authority… the adult can't be rigidly arbitrary, but must give the impression of being so much under authority himself that the children sense it and understand that he, too, has things he has to comply with. In other words, they need to see that the rules weren't made for the adult's convenience. (I'm assuming that everyone who is entrusted with the teaching of children recognizes that we are all under God's authority.)"

Children in this stage of development are exerting initiative, according to Erikson's Stages of Psychosocial Development. They start thinking of their own games, their own play scenarios, their own projects. They want to help you bake and clean, and they ask a lot of questions. This is why this is the key time to teach good habits and expectations. At their core, they are asking, "If I do this, is it okay?" Preschool environments interfere not only with the development of Godly character, but they interfere with a child's initiative. At home, children have a great deal of control over their own environments and there is the possibility of engaging in many child-initiated activities. In a classroom, most of the time is planned by the teacher and child-initiated activities are frowned on. A child who successfully navigates through this stage has a well-developed sense of purpose and is prepared for the next stage, dubbed industry, which starts at about age six. A child who is frustrated in his efforts feels guilty for trying and is ripe for later development of anxiety and depression.

The way that children learn what is expected of them and how to respond is through repetitive social situations called frames, according to Dr. David Elkind. Each frame has its own rules, expectations, and understandings, for example, getting ready for bed or visiting grandma. Children have to learn an enormous number of frames and learn them in a particular order because many of them build on each other (for example, an infant must learn eating and playing frames before he can learn family meal and "friend game" frames). These frames are learned through regular family routines, habits, moral training, and play. They are essential to understanding and navigating the world, and they are primarily learned before age seven.

The major psychosocial developmental task of six- to twelve-year-olds is industry, as I mentioned above. I will only touch on it here since much of this stage falls to the older child. A child needs to feel competent and confident in his abilities. He needs to feel that he can contribute something. The important thing to remember about this stage in relation to young children is that very often, young children are given tasks to do that they cannot possibly succeed at because they are not developmentally ready. This contributes to feelings not of competence, but helplessness and inferiority.

The Brain Creates Itself

In *Endangered Minds* by Dr. Jane Healy, an educational psychologist and educator for more than 40 years who has won the Delta Kappa Gamma Society International Educator Award, writes that the brain seeks what it needs when it needs it. It goes through stages of development in which it will be ready for that new thing it wasn't ready for before. Elkind refers to this as the *structural imperative.* He writes, "The structural imperative is one form of intrinsic motivation that derives from children's need to realize an intellectual potential or mental structure." Trying to force the brain to do things before it is ready will result in inadequate development and compensatory connections that are less than optimal.

In other words, the brain demands the type of stimulation necessary to form the next mental structure. One example is language. Another is a stage of mental development called concrete operations, which is essential to formal learning (we will talk more about this in the next chapter). Concrete operational thinking involves the understanding of rule-based learning and behavior, such as "when two vowels go walking, the first does the talking," group games, and conservation of number. However, this stage is not attained by doing math worksheets at age five or teaching reading to four-year-olds. This is yet another reason why it is essential not to push our own agenda on young children. Forcing young children to do such things only contributes to feelings of inferiority and helplessness. If they are able to do these things only when forced, their learning will be less than optimal and, most likely, will not include real understanding, but only rote memorization.

It is profound to consider the fact that the brain essentially creates itself. It knows what it needs. I prefer, though, to think of it as God being the artist behind the one-of-a-kind canvas of each individual's brain. When the foundational layer of paint has dried, only then does the Great Artist add the next layer. If someone other than the artist comes along and adds some paint here and there because she is impatient to see the finished masterpiece, the painting may not be completely ruined, but the artist will need to scrape away this added paint. Sometimes, the artist will alter the intended vision for the painting in order to accommodate the flaws created by the untrained passerby. Sometimes, the added paint cannot be completely removed, and the finished masterpiece is flawed because of it. Do we trust the Great Artist to add in the next layers of paint or do we get impatient to see the masterpiece and try to add in our own splotches of color?

There have been times when I have really blown it in encouraging initiative and industry, especially with my two oldest. Tiger wanted to wash dishes, but spilled water all over the floor. She wanted to help me bake but often dumped flour and eggs everywhere. When they were toddlers, I allowed them free reign over the house and made sure that the low shelves did not have anything dangerous and breakable. But, then, when they were three- to five-years-old, I said no—a lot. Hawk went through with his ideas in spite of me, but Tiger slumped her shoulders and walked away. I hated cleaning up messes and felt like a maid because I spent a lot of time cleaning. I discouraged anything that added to the mess. I am ashamed to say that not only did I often discourage Tiger's initiative, but I also asked her to take on responsibilities that she probably wasn't ready for. Little kids can learn to help, but it is hard to teach them when you also have a toddler and maybe even a baby.

Hawk liked to disappear. There were several AMBER alerts for him when he was little. Once, at a museum, I bent down to help Tiger tie her shoes, Butterfly was in her stroller, and Hawk ran off. I brought the girls with me to each exhibit area but asked Tiger to stay with

Butterfly while I searched around and between the kiosks. I had to move quickly because Hawk ran everywhere and snuck around. This scenario happened multiple times over the years, even when he reached his teens. Tiger learned how to care for her siblings at a younger age than she really should have.

This happened academically sometimes too. Instead of looking to God, I looked at other homeschoolers and scope-and-sequence charts. As I mentioned earlier, I had a lot of fear, and fear drove me to do things that weren't healthy for me or my children. Thank the Lord Jesus that he brought me out of that place so my children could develop as he designed them to. He showed me that He designed us to walk through these stages in our spiritual life, too.

First, we must trust that He is our Savior. We must have faith because that is the only path to salvation: "I am the way, the truth, and the life, no one comes to the Father except through me." (John 14:6). Then, through our faith, we are empowered to control our flesh impulses: "What a wretched man I am! Who will rescue me from this body of death? Thanks be to God—through Jesus Christ our Lord!" (Romans 7:24-25). We learn to talk to our Heavenly Father and ask questions through prayer: "Do not be anxious about anything, but in everything, by prayer and petition, with thanksgiving, present your requests to God. And the peace of God, which transcends all understanding will guard your hearts and your minds in Christ." (Philippians 4:6-7).

We become part of a body of believers, of which we are essential members: "For by the grace given me I say to every one of you: do not think of yourself more highly than you ought, but rather think of yourself with sober judgement in accordance with the measure of faith that God has given you. Just as each of us has one body with many members, and these members do not all have the same function, so in Christ we who are many form one body, and each member belongs to all the others." (Romans 12:3-5).

As we grow and learn and read our Bibles, we begin to be able to discern God's Will for our lives and understand that He does not ask us to do anything for which He has not already equipped us: "Scripture is God-breathed and is useful for teaching, rebuking, correcting and training in righteousness so that the man of God may be thoroughly equipped for every good work." (2 Timothy 3:16). Through our children's developmental stages, we can get a clearer picture of our spiritual growth and are prepared to teach to them the biblical truths that we are also bound to obey.

Lots of Time to Play

In addition to invaluable lessons about good/bad, right/wrong, and true/false that are learned through family life, a young child learns a great deal through play. I have been able to see that if young children are not required to do anything except perhaps help with chores, they will spend 75 percent of their time in play. The other 25 percent would be eating, reading books, art activities (which could also be play), or asking questions and discussing with you. Play is the main way that children exercise initiative, and we need to respect their efforts to protect, defend, and enhance their sense of competence through play. We need to be careful not to manipulate their play to get more math education into their day or to teach some creative skill.

Play is more than making ourselves feel powerful, though. It is essential for proper brain development. Dr. Stuart Brown, founder of the National Institute for Play, has plenty to say about the benefits of play in his book *Play: How it Shapes the Brain, Opens the Imagination, and Invigorates the Soul.* He cites one researcher that showed that active play stimulates nerve growth in the areas of the brain where emotions and executive decisions are processed. The time in our lives when we play the most correlates to when our frontal lobes are developing the fastest. Play activity actually helps sculpt the brain.

We should not underestimate the importance of play in a child's life. For it to be most beneficial, it must be active, open-ended play in which the child must act on his environment, not simply watch the toy move around. Through play, we create simulations of life without actually having to experience them so we can learn lessons and skills without being at risk. In play, we create new, imaginative, cognitive combinations, and through these combinations, we find what works. Play is crucial to healthy development and the benefits will later show themselves in the growing child's ability to use their creativity to solve problems, invent, and think critically.

Because of the prevalence of video and computer games, robots and other electronic toys, and iPads, I feel I must define what "play" really is. The more the child has to do himself, the better the toy. If the child has to physically build it, mold it, move it, provide the sounds, imagine it, create it, etc., then it is true play. Pressing buttons is not playing, even if it is moving a remote-controlled car. Minecraft is not true playing, even though the child is creating. It is definitely a step up from computer games, but the child is not acting on his environment in the same way as he is when he builds with Legos, K'Nex, or ZomeTools.

Play equipment need not be elaborate or expensive. We do not throw out boxes at my house. They don't have to be large boxes, just boxes from book or grocery deliveries. Both Hawk and Mouse salivate at the site of empty boxes and immediately ask for shipping tape and a sharp object. It doesn't take long before a new castle, secret hideout, ship, or squirrel hut appears in my living room. They also save their money to buy clay, fabric scraps, and small wood pieces. Pretty soon, little potion bottles and tiny animals cover my table, complete with their own clothes and furniture. All you need are the raw materials. For little children, that might be clay, blocks, sand, dolls, boxes, basic toy cars, and large swaths of cloth, such as play silks. There are an infinite number of possibilities for children to use their minds to transform the raw materials into their dreams.

Appropriate Learning

Young children do not learn the same way as adults and children aged eight and older. They ask many questions, often beginning with "Why?" Note that they aren't really asking for the scientific answer to why the sky looks blue but rather the *purpose* of it being blue. This parallels their need to know that they have purpose, too. This is part of their drive to initiate. It is to know that they and everything else has purpose. These children sound more sophisticated than they really are and it is sometimes, but not always, useful to answer their questions with additional questions, even if it is to ask them to answer their own question ("Why do you think it is blue?"). They can be challenged by elaborating on what they already know, such as learning the names of other animals that live in the sea besides fish. They are not usually capable of understanding totally new and abstract concepts that they have not experienced firsthand.

At this age, everything is learned through their senses and pictorial representation of what they experience through their senses. They are able to combine sensory experiences of say, being on a boat, fishing in the lake, with an experience of wading in a river to arrive at the idea that you can swim and fish in bodies of water. But then, they may erroneously think that there should be fish in a swimming pool. Everything is in the eternal now for them, and that is why they have difficulty with transitions and with waiting for things. They may remember things that happened in the past. As memories are tied to language, their memories tend to be associated with emotion or sensation. Ask a three-year-old what he did 2 days ago, and he most likely can't tell you. Ask a seven-year-old, and he probably can.

Young children learn best through projects, activities, and frames. These might be cooking soup, making people with playdough, growing flowers, putting on a puppet show, or building a sandcastle. These are all activities that are easily done as a family and fit nicely with an unschooling lifestyle.

Not only do young children learn differently, but their brains just aren't developed enough to do the same tasks that they will be able to do if given two to five additional years. A child cannot think logically and rationally until they are around seven-years-old. Until that time, young children engage in magical thinking and do not learn from the written word; they only learn through their senses. Perhaps that is why Hawk did not believe me when I told him that he should not put his tongue in the electrical outlet because he would be electrocuted. He didn't know what being electrocuted was, as he had never experienced it. So, he picked at the safety plug, and before I knew it, Hawk sat there screaming in pain, his tongue hanging out of his mouth. I guess God still has plans for his life.

While age seven may seem to be a bit old for formal learning tasks, there is a great body of evidence that suggests that formal learning should come even later. Research conducted by Dr. Raymond and Dorothy Moore, sifting through eight thousand studies (no, that is not a typo!), found that neurophysiologists and learning psychologists arrived independently at the same ages—about eight to ten years—as ideal for the beginning of school tasks. They also found that vision, hearing, and, to some extent, maternal deprivation also converged on the eight-to-ten age range. They have a term for this called the Integrated Maturity Level. "This is the point at which the developmental variables of affective, psychomotor, perceptual, and cognitive within the child reach an optimum peak of readiness in maturation and cooperative functioning for typical school experiences." In other words, the child's emotions, body, mind, eyes, ears, sociability, and more are not sufficiently matured for formal learning until the child is *at least* eight years old.

We have to remember that the ages cited above are a range, but generally the range of developmental readiness tends toward the higher end of the spectrum, not the lower end. Children also develop asynchronously, or unevenly, across different areas. Both of my daughters' language abilities developed early, along with some of their reasoning and planning skills. However, Tiger's mathematical reasoning ability came later. That was a source of frustration for me. She didn't understand algebraic concepts until her late teens, while Hawk, as I mentioned earlier, breezed through algebra in 4 months at fifteen. But, Hawk had troubles of his own. While he learned to speak at a normal age, his reading and vocabulary skills didn't really take off until he turned twelve. However, he was able to swing on the swing set when he was two and take apart battery-powered toys when he was four. Butterfly's reading and math abilities have followed the average timetable. But Mouse, who has an enormous vocabulary for his age and began learning to read at age five, plateaued after a year. His attention to detail and ability to create sewing machines and moving assembly lines with Legos began at age five. Every child has his own timetable for normal development that needs to be respected. Even if there is a medical problem (such as vision, hearing, Down's syndrome, etc.), we need to wait for his brain to ask for the next skill to be developed.

Importance of Movement and Nature

In addition to appropriate learning strategies, children need to move. This may seem obvious in light of recent statistics about the health of our youth, but there are even more important reasons to get children moving. Dr. Carla Hannaford, an award-winning neurophysiologist and author of *Smart Moves: Why Learning is Not All in Your Head*, says, "movement awakens and activates many of our mental capacities.

Movement integrates and anchors new information and experience into our neural networks. Movement is vital to all the actions by which we embody and express our learning, our understanding, and ourselves." Dr. John Ratey, professor of psychiatry at Harvard Medical School and author of several books including *Spark: The Revolutionary New Science of Exercise and the Brain*, agrees. He writes "exercise improves learning on three levels: first, it optimizes your mind-set to improve alertness, attention, and motivation; second, it prepares and encourages nerve cells to bind to one another, which is the cellular basis for logging in new information; and third, it spurs the development of new nerve cells from stem cells in the hippocampus."

Hannaford also asserts that in order to wake up our brains, we must move. This is most evident in children who have trouble focusing on tasks that they need to do or intend to do. Dr. Ratey explains that these children improve with a combination of complex movements in the midst of heavy exertion, such as in martial arts, gymnastics, figure skating, ballet, rock climbing, mountain biking, or even skateboarding. These sports combine acute stress, which is the fight-or-flight response, and executive function skills. This puts the brain on high alert and turns on the reward center, which motivates and helps these kids focus. Exercise is essential to helping these children develop better self-control and attention skills, because it increases the levels of two important neurotransmitters—dopamine and norepinephrine—and their receptor sites and increases growth of the cerebellum. This area of the brain and the previously mentioned neurotransmitters are what enable all of us to be calm and focused.

I saw some of these benefits in my younger children. I enrolled Mouse in parkour because he voiced that he hates sports, but I knew that it's bad for children to sit around all day, even if they are not in front of screens. With his sensory issues and other difficulties, I hoped that the rigor of parkour would help. Getting him there often involved much advance preparation and ignoring his negativity. I saw firsthand how complex movements benefitted him. His mood improved, he tolerated frustration better, and he met boys who later became good friends.

One of the challenges of Asperger's is difficulty with coordinated body movements, and I saw this with Butterfly. Out of all of my children, she took the longest to learn to ride a bicycle and to swim. While her siblings rode at around five years old, she couldn't ride until she was seven. She struggled with traditional group swim lessons. The instructors thought she didn't pay attention when the problem really stemmed from her Asperger's. In addition, her tentativeness around playground equipment and anxiety around certain types of play activities told me that she may need some help. She participated in one-on-one swim lessons and then learned quickly. I enrolled her in two movement classes with the special recreation division of our park district. Her anxiety largely disappeared, and a few years later, she won first place in her division for gymnastics at the Illinois State Special Olympics.

Movement is necessary not just to improve our learning and grow smarter brains, but, in order to express what we have learned, we must move in some way, whether that is moving our mouths as we talk about it, moving our hands to write about it, or moving our entire bodies to imitate it. Hannaford even goes so far as to say that, without movement, there is no conscious thought. We can confirm this with ourselves when we remember that we pace when we are deep in thought or we get our best ideas when we are running. So it is with our children. One easy way to incorporate movement is through hands-on learning. Hannaford explains that "whenever touch is combined with the other senses, much more of the brain is activated, thus building more complex nerve networks and tapping into more learning potential."

Hands-on learning integrates all the senses, making it the ideal way for this age group to learn. For Butterfly, touching was understanding, and I let her touch everything that I could. All my reading about

Asperger's told me that she learned best through concrete, sensory experiences. Little did I know that, in fact, *all* children learn that way before age eight. Thank goodness that I emphasized sensory-based learning for her two older siblings, too. There are no learning styles at this time of a child's life. That comes later.

After reading about the importance of movement to brain development, you may be tempted to sign your five-year-old up for Little League. However, most organized sports do not keep children moving in a variety of ways in the same way that unfettered, outdoor time can. In watching Hawk play summer baseball when he was nine, I have seen that there is a great deal of standing around and waiting. Even in winter basketball, he would play for 5 minutes, racing around the court, and then he would sit for 10 minutes. He would play for another 5 minutes and then sit again. For movement to be truly beneficial, it has to be more sustained, and as noted above, the more complex, the better. Activities such as playing on playground equipment for 1 or 2 hours, family bike rides for half an hour to an hour at a reasonable pace, group games such as the perennial favorite, Tag, keep kids moving for more than 5 minutes at a time.

My personal favorite is to get my children out in a wild natural setting, such as a forest preserve. Out there, not only do you get the benefits of movement, you also get some added benefits. Richard Louv, who has appeared on several talk shows, has written seven books about family and nature, and is the chairman of The Children and Nature Network, writes in his book *Last Child in the Woods* that time spent in nature protects children from depression, improves their attention span, offers fodder for imagination, and engages all their senses. Dr. and Dorothy Moore write in their book *The Successful Homeschool Family Handbook* that being outside makes children more cooperative, calm, and ready for concentration on mental tasks. Time in the natural world also teaches that simulations of nature in museums, books, zoos, and even restaurants pale in comparison to the real thing. Louv writes "any natural place contains a reservoir of information, and therefore the potential for inexhaustible new discoveries."

Looking at a snake in a book is not the same as seeing a real snake slither across a trail. Watching birds in a pet store is not the same as spying them in the tops of trees in the wild. All of creation teaches us about the glory of God. In Job 12:7-10, Job said, "But ask the animals, and they will teach you, or the birds of the air, and they will tell you; or speak to the earth, and it will teach you, or let the fish of the sea inform you. Which of these does not know that the of the Lord has done this? In his hand is the life of every creature and the breath of all mankind." God reveals Himself to us through His creation, and we can learn about Him from it, as it says in Romans 1:20, "For since the creation of the world God's invisible qualities—his eternal power and divine nature— have been clearly seen, being understood from what has been made, so that men are without excuse." Children learn about their Lord from nature, too.

Experiences Teaching Small Children

In addition to being a teacher's aide in conventional preschools, I have participated in homeschool co-ops off and on and have taught several classes to both the younger and older age groups. My observations bear witness to what the Moores say about development of young children. I have learned while teaching at the co-op that children under eight years really are not capable of much formal learning. Many of them struggle with basic fine motor skills. Others have a very short attention span. Still others have trouble focusing when they are part of group settings or just in general (oddball statements such as "me and my grandpa went fishing last year" frequently interrupt the flow of a lesson, which just demonstrates that children this age are more in tune with their emotions and concrete life experiences than they are with anything else). It often takes them 40 minutes just to color, cut, and paste a simple activity.

I have also taught preschool Sunday School at two different churches. I have not taught this age group in years because it is very frustrating. It took a long time to get everyone seated and quiet. Very often, the children talked at the same time I tried to teach them about Bible stories from the chosen curriculum. They couldn't sit still, and when they raised their hands to answer a question, they almost always said, "Jesus!" This made it obvious that they weren't really listening. Many of the children struggled to cut and paste, and sometimes there were issues with inappropriate touching between children. Sometimes, we just showed a Veggie Tales video. I wondered how much these kids actually learned about sin, forgiveness, God's love, and faith.

Trying to *teach* anything to children this age and expecting them to retain it is a waste of time. I don't mean that it is a waste of time to do anything with them; I mean that trying to get them to *book-learn* is a waste of time. They only learn through concrete experiences, and they can only handle the contrived type in bite-size pieces (as in a *hands-on* classroom experience). I have seen this repeated over and over as each of my children have passed through this stage. There is great wisdom in waiting until the child has mastered basic fine motor skills, his nervous system has developed enough that he can hear and see and attend to a task for more than 2 minutes, and his mind has matured enough that he is interested in more than his own life experiences and can retain what he learns.

I have to admit that before my teaching experience, I was a bit skeptical of what Dr. Raymond and Dorothy Moore said about children under the age of ten. I doubted that it was really wise to wait that long to teach them formal studies. Isn't my child capable of learning many things before age ten? Then I thought about it. Most of the information (and even life experiences) that I remember happened after age eight. Most of that information was taught in repetitive cycles over my school age years. Perhaps that is the only reason anything is remembered at all.

So What Do We Do all Day

You are probably wondering what you're supposed to do all day with your three- to eight-year-old children if you're not writing lesson plans, not following a curriculum, not insisting they learn academic skills, and you are allowing them to pursue their own interests (which may at times mean that they play most of the day). In addition to the items I mentioned earlier, I suggest blocks, plants and animals, books, music, dramatic play, art materials, carpentry, water table and other science exploration tools, instruments, sandbox, riding toys, playground equipment, and project-oriented, parent-/teacher-led activities.

It really is that simple. Whatever parent-led activities you do should be brief and about things with which they are familiar, such as animals or plants from their backyards. Charlotte Mason has a list of attainments for six-year-olds that includes the following: to be able to recite poems, parables, songs, Bible stories; to be able to describe accurately various natural environments and walks they've been on; to be able to identify birds, flowers, leaves; to tell three stories about their pets; to be able to do basic handiwork; and a few other things that are disputable such as being able to copy letters from a book and do simple addition and subtraction using counters. These abilities are fairly easy to attain just by taking your child on walks around the neighborhood or the zoo, planting a garden (even if it's a potted garden on a balcony), keeping pets, and reading the Bible to your child.

But, you say, we aren't going to do that every day. What do we do with all that time? Well, what do you want to do all day that isn't lazy or selfish? What does God want you to do all day that gives glory to Him? What has God put inside of you as a unique package of interests, talents, and skills that are to be used for His purposes? Chances are that some of these things can be done at home with children alongside you. After all, He gave you your children because there is something in you that He wants you to pass on to them.

You might begin with a very basic plan of your day: breakfast, lunch, and dinner, along with the time it takes to prepare each of those meals. What else do you want to do with your children that honors God, your child, and gives you joy? Bible time? Worship? Read-aloud time? Outdoor time? Quiet time? Pick one or two other hooks on which to build your day. The times in between might be filled with household chores that you do together or assign. It might be filled with baking cookies together, visiting an elderly neighbor or relative, visiting the library, or building a birdhouse. The key is to fill your days with meaningful, real experiences that involve you, your children, and the community as you deem appropriate. Remember, children of this age learn best from projects, routines, and activities that have meaning through a personal relationship or experience. Don't forget lots of time to just play.

Is sitting at a desk, listening to a teacher drone on about some detached topic, an experience? No. The kind of experience I am talking about is experience that is born out of active participation in a relationship the child cares about. If you are nurturing your child's soul by inviting her into your life, your interests, and honoring her interests and developmental needs, you are building for your family an authentic life born of real experiences. These real experiences can be with great books, great people, or great places. If the child cares about the main character in a book, the story will shape his life in a way he will never forget. If the child cares about the people in her life, she will carry that love to the world and change it for the better. If the child experiences great places, she will see God and know him better. The relationships a child has with books, with the world around him, and with the people in his life will determine how and whether a child learns through his experiences with them.

Here are some ideas on how you might incorporate some meaningful experiences based on family interests.

Music/art Teach your children some favorite songs or fingerplays. Create artistic dances with scarves or other props. Borrow some new CDs from the library and play them in the background. See if your children can drum to the beat of the songs. Write some new songs of your own, and all of you can sing them and play basic rhythm for them. Learn to paint or draw, and create a collection of nature drawings or of your own children. What a treasure! Write some new stories or plays for the children to listen to or act out together. Make puppets and put on a puppet show with or for the children. Learn a new craft together, and make items for gifts, for your children, or for sale.

Nature/Science Plant and tend a garden of flowers and/or vegetables. Take the kids on nature hikes, fishing trips, kite flying, camping trips, zoos, farms, etc. Start an insect collection. Have pets. Keep a nature journal yourself, and let them see you making notes in it. They can at least try to draw what they see if they are unable to write notes. Let them help you cook and bake (chemistry). Let them help you preserve food, learn to make soda pop, cheese, and other goodies (more chemistry). Watch the weather reports together, or keep a weather calendar. Take them out late at night to look at the stars and the moon. Have tools such as insect nets, field guides, rock hammers, and more on hand to encourage them to explore God's creation. This area is one of the easiest to do with kids because, if you just get them outside in an unmanicured lawn or other wilder place, they will discover plenty about creation, but be sure to explore, too, and ask questions.

History/geography With this age group, it can be hard to do geography beyond your own neighborhood. Unless you travel broadly and regularly with your children, they may not show much interest in different people and places that are foreign to them. A six- or seven-year-old is beginning to understand his place in the wider world and may be interested in looking at a globe, but don't push this. It is more important that a young child feels comfortable in his own neighborhood and town and knows a bit about how to get around in that town. Going on errands with you accomplishes this very nicely. You might also try letterboxing (see www.letterboxing.org). However, they might be interested in other places in the world if you cook foods from other places. Take them to interesting ethnic restaurants, and do some ethnic crafts with them. Read stories about famous Americans. Start a family genealogy project.

Math/reading Be careful not to push in these areas just because the neighborhood kids can read and know all their math facts by age eight. Play games together that use mathematical and reading skills but don't overdo it. They can see you measuring, counting, making lists, reading books, comparing prices, counting money, telling time, writing letters, and more in your everyday activities so they know that these skills are important for everyday life. If you ask questions of them while you are using these skills, especially when cooking, shopping, telling time, it will help them to develop their skills. You can also have them dictate their stories to you, and they can create little books of their own stories that way.

The important points to remember about this age group are that you are not doing them a disservice by allowing them extra time to play and create rather than do worksheets. You are giving them a gift. Early academics do not produce later success. Quite the opposite is often true. If you want to give your child a head-start on his future, follow your instincts. Remember, "If any one of you thinks he is wise by the standards of this age, he should become a fool so that he may become wise. For the wisdom of this world is foolishness in God's sight." (I Corinthians 3:18-19).

Study Questions

1. What myths have you believed about young children?

2. How are you doing in leading an unhurried life?

3. Are there regrets about this period in your child's life? How can you remedy this?

4. How have your beliefs about play and movement been challenged?

5. List some ideas on how to spend your days with your young child.

Chapter 4

Thoughts on Teaching
Children Aged Eight to Twelve

A s each of my children passed out of the magical stage of early childhood, I saw a distinct change in their thinking, their habits, their play, and their overall competence. They asked questions like, "What difference does it make if I spend my screen time watching television or playing on the computer? They're both screens, right? At least in a computer game, I'm doing something." Uggh. Got me there. It is during this stage that they start to question the assertion that there is a Santa Claus and a Tooth Fairy. They say things like, "We don't have a chimney. How does he get in? Why would you leave the door unlocked? You always say we have to lock the door at night to keep burglars out." They remember visiting a museum 2 months, or a year, before and can recount details you have forgotten. Their academic skills are still developing, but they are beginning to show a preference for how they like to learn. In addition, boys demonstrate a desire for competition in their training, while girls continue to prefer a more relational learning model. For more details about these differences, please check out *Why Gender Matters* by Leonard Sax, a psychologist and medical doctor who speaks all over the world on gender and parenting issues. It is very valuable for better understanding the special academic challenges of this age group.

While children in this age group often still suffer from ill-placed expectations, we often underestimate them in other areas. Cognitive skills won't be fully developed for almost a decade, but they can develop their sense of industry through other means, such as service and entrepreneurship. If young children have developed a strong set of virtues, those virtues will be solidified and put into practice during this stage of their lives. They don't need constant reminders of what you expect of them, what the rules are. They are ready to serve others and learn rule-based behavior in their play activities and otherwise.

Service

Service to others can be a powerful motivator. More importantly, it helps the growing child develop a sense of competence. If you remember from the last chapter, around age six or seven, a child enters a development stage where he learns that he is capable and competent or he learns helplessness. This stage ends when the child is approximately thirteen. How does a child learn competence through service? Through serving others, he learns in a non-threatening but meaningful way that he can do things that make a difference in the lives of other people, even if it's just bringing a smile to an elderly woman's face. It adds a new dimension to their sense of belonging not just to a family or peer group, but also to the community and wider world. It helps them see the true meaning of what Christ told the Pharisees, "'Love the Lord your God with all your heart and with all your soul and with all your mind.' This is the first and greatest commandment. And the second is like it: '*Love your neighbor as yourself.*' All the Law and the Prophets hang on these two commandments." (Matthew 22: 37-40).

Our purpose is to love God and love people. In an unschooling home in which your days are not filled with curriculum, there is more time to be involved with your community and demonstrate the love of Christ to others. Children can put this into action by helping elderly neighbors or nursing home residents, by doing extra chores around the house or helping younger siblings, caring for you when you are sick, and, as they approach eleven or twelve, do much more. They can volunteer in animal shelters, sometimes at veterinary hospitals, junior-high mission trips through the church, assisting at vacation Bible school or Sunday school, mother's helpers, and whatever else they or you can dream up. Don't be afraid to ask people. Let children choose what kind of service they'd like to do, especially as they get older. When they are young, you need to be the one bringing them along with you as you do service.

A special note: Because of the heightened ability to think rationally, children this age are very intolerant of double standards. You *must* practice what you preach.

Another benefit of service is that it "brings nobility and self-respect no other activity can match... It thrives on initiative and nurtures creativity," according to Dr. Raymond and Dorothy Moore in their book *The Successful Homeschool Family Handbook*. The Moore couple service with manual labor and believe that entrepreneurship should also be encouraged. We will discuss that in a bit. Service builds character, selflessness, and better relationships between themselves and all whom they come in contact with. They learn how to see needs in their community and strive to fill those needs. They feel needed, useful, and gain empathy. It helps them connect with others and learn more about themselves in the process.

Service has always been important to me but difficult to do with young children. The best I could do was make an occasional meal for a new mom, someone with long-term illness, or a hurting family. As my children grew up, I looked for other possibilities we could do together. Visiting the elderly seemed like the best option, even though my heart is with unwed mothers/abortion prevention. Little Brothers Friends of the Elderly (LBFE), which is an organization dedicated to addressing loneliness in the elderly, seemed like a good fit, and they had a variety of ways to serve. My children and I enjoyed bringing birthday presents and Christmas gifts to elderly men and women for a few years.

After a few years, serving the elderly felt more like an obligation than a joy and, sometimes, we had to go to crime-ridden neighborhoods. I didn't want to endanger my children. We stopped volunteering with LBFE, and I concentrated on serving my own church for a while. When Mouse turned six, we discovered Feed My Starving Children, and it was a natural fit for our family. I wanted the children to see serving as fun and rewarding, not a toilsome obligation. Getting Mouse to serve cheerfully was a triumph in itself. We also found a local organization dedicated to setting up service projects for families, and we learned how to recycle plastic bags into sleeping quilts for the homeless.

When Tiger was ten, she began volunteering on her own at an animal shelter. As she got older, she found that she really enjoyed working with small children and volunteered at the library's story hour and at the Morton Arboretum's Children's Garden. Then, she moved on to working with small children at our church. Now that Butterfly is older, she also regularly volunteers at church with Vacation Bible School (VBS) and Sunday School. Hawk has dander and environmental allergies so working with animals was out of the question for him. His service came later, in high school, when he helped in the craft room for VBS, went on a mission trip, and served several years as a Science Achiever at the Museum of Science and Industry.

Entrepreneurship

Before the Industrial Age, children always worked alongside their parents and made important contributions to the family's income through their efforts. Even when factories began to dot the landscape, children still contributed to the family income, providing as much as 20 percent, until child labor laws were enacted. I'm not suggesting that your eight-year-old should be cleaning toilets at the local restaurant, but what I'm getting at is that children in the eight to twelve age range that we are talking about are capable of learning to do meaningful work. Usually, this means handicrafts such as simple carpentry, whittling, quilting, weaving, or crochet, for example. It may also include cooking, shoveling snow, raking leaves, growing food, pulling weeds, and the like. The Apostle Paul says in 1 Thessalonians 4:11, "Make it your ambition to lead a quiet life, to mind your own business and to work with your hands, just as we told you, so that your daily life may win the respect of outsiders and so that you will not be dependent on anybody." He further says in Ephesians that we must work, doing something with our own hands, so that we may have something to share with those in need (Ephesians 3:28).

Children can gain a sense of competence and usefulness through learning manual skills during this time so that they can learn to be independent and have something to offer others. Chris Mercogliano, teacher and administrator at the Albany Free School since 1973, writes in *In Defense of Childhood* "we seem to have forgotten that meaningful, interesting work is an organic part of young people's instinctive movement toward self-sufficiency and independence." Dr. Raymond and Dorothy Moore agree. They write in *The Successful Homeschool Family Handbook* that many institutions show that the "balancing and invigorating effect of developing creativity and using manual skills endows students and adults with unusual leadership." It seems that it is not a lengthy list of academic achievements and extracurricular activities that helps a child become a leader in society, but rather good, old-fashioned manual labor and selflessness toward others.

John Taylor Gatto said at the InHome Homeschool Conference in March 2010 that he interviewed admissions officers at Ivy League Schools to find out what distinguished one applicant from another since they all had high SAT scores, perfect GPAs, etc. What they told him was they were looking for evidence that a student would become someone of eminence. How did they know who would become someone of eminence? They looked for students who had started businesses, made some significant contribution to their community, or had done something extraordinary at considerable risk to themselves (such as hike from the tip of South America all the way up to Alaska). He was not talking about eight- to twelve-year-olds, but teenagers. However, the principles still apply to this age group because it establishes early patterns of confidence and self-reliance. As homeschoolers (and especially unschoolers), we have time on our side. Instead of signing our children up for all the same extracurricular activities and classes that public-schooled children are in, we have the chance to cultivate real character, skill, confidence, leadership, and independence through family entrepreneurship and service.

I have always encouraged my children to be industrious and creative, regularly talking about starting businesses. When Hawk and Tiger were young, they washed the neighbors' cars, walked dogs, and made homemade chocolate candies to sell. When Tiger turned twelve, she had opportunities through our homeschool support group to babysit and be a teacher's aide for childcare during a women's Bible study. Then, I discovered a Children's Christmas Craft Fair, offered by another local homeschool group. At first, Hawk and Butterfly participated, making clay figurines and doll quilts to sell. They did very well and chose to do it the following year also. The third year, Mouse joined them and sold felted animals. He also sold a lot of product. Then, the group didn't offer it anymore, but Hawk was then old enough to shovel snow and worked with a homeschooling dad for two winters. As I mentioned at the beginning of the book, he also entered an Entrepreneur Academy offered by a local library and won second place in their competition.

Play and Movement

As previously stated, children at this age are more capable of rule-based behavior and, therefore, tend to enjoy group games based on rules. These are the years that children typically become interested in sports or group games, such as Tag and dodgeball, and can learn choreographed movements such as dance and martial arts. Even though social games tend to take more precedence at this time, children are still using their imaginations. According to Dr. Stuart Brown, imagination continues to nourish the spirit and "throughout life, remains a key to emotional resilience and creativity." Creative, imaginative play takes on new meaning during this time because of children's increasing ability to understand their world. It becomes valuable as a means to "bend the reality of our ordinary lives, and in the process, germinate new ideas and ways of being... Creative play takes our minds to places we have never been, pioneering new paths that the real world can follow." (Brown)

Play becomes more sophisticated. Entire worlds are created, destroyed, and made new again. There is no more playing kitchen, no more just pretending to be mommies, fairies, firemen, or knights. Now, the girls have involved storylines about being best friends who live across the country and haven't seen each other in years. Now the boys are fighting epic battles where they have to watch out for evil lords in neighboring kingdoms. At this age, the boys may also engage in rougher play. Don't be alarmed. According to research, this is necessary for the development of social awareness, cooperation, fairness, and altruism. Engaging in this type of play has been shown to actually help your son control violent impulses later in life and is beneficial to hyperactive boys in learning how to control impulsiveness. When each of my sons turned ten, they couldn't wait to play paintball. Hawk's first experience left him with a badly bruised back since one kid kept shooting him point blank. The boys were more sportsmanlike when Mouse went for the first time. Did Hawk avoid playing again? Not a chance. He bragged about how tough he was to put up with them and complained about what jerks they were. He felt it his duty to protect his brother when he was old enough to go and made armor for them both.

Even though our children are getting older, they still need plenty of playtime. Depriving children of playtime can stunt their brain growth and may impair the maturation of executive function skills. Learning happens best when children (and adults) are allowed to play with ideas through pretending or discussion or creating something, as this involves more of the brain than just sitting and listening to a lecture or filling in the blanks on a worksheet.

Children this age also continue to need plenty of physical movement, just as when they were younger. It is essential to their ability to mentally focus, to exercise motor skills, to be emotionally stable, and to develop social skills. Everything stated about the benefits of movement in the last chapter applies here as well. Children move because they were never meant to sit in a chair for long hours. We would do well to follow their example.

Appropriate Learning

As discussed in the previous chapter, around age seven, and most fully by age eight, your child has reached an important milestone in his cognitive development. He can now think more logically about concrete events, although he will still have trouble with hypothetical or abstract events. His use of logic is limited, however, to inductive logic—going from a specific experience to a general principle. This is why he can learn more quickly about the consequences of his behavior and sometimes only needs one or two experiences before he understands. He can conceptualize learning, he can understand rule-based behavior and learning, and he can apply his mind to anything that he can see with his eyes or that he can see in his mind's eye. He most likely cannot yet work on problems that require deductive logic or that require an understanding of the abstract. He will remain in this stage of development until he is about twelve years old, or sometimes longer. His new cognitive abilities, called concrete operational, dovetail nicely with his stage of development according to Erikson's Stages of Psychosocial Development. Between the ages of six or seven and about age twelve, a child is working to develop a sense of competence, or industry. If his cognitive abilities are respected and he is encouraged to pursue meaningful tasks that he can succeed at, he will attain a sense of competence. Service and entrepreneurship, as discussed above, are powerful ways to help your child in this.

Math, Reading, and Writing

Reading, writing, and arithmetic are essential skills that are usually emphasized at this point in a child's life. Schools spend inordinate amounts of time on these skill areas, and sometimes, we as homeschoolers do the same thing. However, these are skills that cannot be taught until the child is developmentally ready. As God has led me on this journey, I have discovered this to be true over and over again. Just as walking and talking are skills that we did not teach, reading, writing, and calculating are skills that we would do well not to teach, at least not until the child shows readiness by asking for it, vehemently. We have to remember God's timing is not the same as the world's timing. Take math, for example. Why do we take six years of a child's life to teach basic arithmetic concepts, at a developmental stage not really suited to abstract thinking? How difficult is it, really, to learn to add, subtract, multiply, and divide whole numbers and non-whole numbers? How hard is it to learn to measure lines and shapes? I would argue that it is not hard at all, if you are between ten and twelve years old or older.

It is amazing that in the late 1920s, a public-school administrator, L. P. Benezet, questioned how math was taught in Manchester, New Hampshire, schools. In the fall of 1929, he chose four schools in neighborhoods where the parents didn't know any English. In those schools, they abandoned all formal instruction in arithmetic below seventh grade. Instead, they concentrated on learning to read, reason, and recite in the English language. At the end of 8 months, he evaluated the children by comparing the experimental group to the traditionally taught students. To summarize what he found, the experimental group was more accurate in estimating distances, reasoning problems, and used more sophisticated words than the traditional group. They read more and had better problem-solving abilities. How can it be that children who are not taught arithmetic actually perform better?

Maybe it's because math is a developmentally based skill and children under age twelve learn it better in context, just like everything else. Math is not divorced from life; it is an integral part of solving everyday problems. Benezet's experiment is not a fluke. The Sudbury Valley School has repeatedly taught nine- to twelve-year-olds K-6 math in *20 contact hours*, no frills or gimmicks, just the desire to learn it. Peter Gray, a professor of psychology at Boston College and Psychology Today blogger, posted on his blog *Freedom to Learn* on April 15, 2010, that he requested stories from real life families who did not teach their children math and examined what happened. He divided the stories into four categories: playful math, instrumental math, didactic math, and college math. What he found was that children learn math concepts best when they are in charge of the learning process, not the teacher/parent, which supports an unschooling lifestyle. The basic concepts are often picked up through play or everyday life activities. Often, it is through games, whether board games, sports, video games, or card games. Outside of this, many of the testimonies showed that if the child saw a need to learn a math concept, even if it was to get into college or for a job, they were very willing to learn it and learned it quickly.

Even mathematicians would not teach math the way that schools teach math, as Paul Lockhart, a mathematician who was a fellow at the Mathematical Sciences Research Institute (MSRI) and assistant professor at Brown University, talks about in his essay *A Mathematician's Lament*. He says, "If I had to design a mechanism for the express purpose of destroying a child's natural curiosity and love of pattern-making, I couldn't possibly do as good a job as is currently being done—I simply wouldn't have the imagination to come up with the kind of senseless, soul-crushing ideas that constitute contemporary mathematics education." So why would we, who have the opportunity to do things differently, imitate the school system? We need to respect our children's developmental timetables and the way that God made them.

We need to talk with our children more about the ways that we use math and how we do it rather than give them superficial worksheets to complete. For example, when my son was six, he could tell you that if he had three cookies and he ate one, there would be two left over. If I tried to "teach" him this on a worksheet, he wouldn't have any idea what I was talking about. I had a game I played with Tiger when she was eight. I gave her five chips and I had eight in my hand (that were hidden from her sight). I took three chips from my hand and put them in view, and then I said to her, "Now I have as many chips in my hand as you have. How many did I have before?" She could always give me the correct answer no matter how I changed the number of chips. But, if I wrote this exchange out in numerical format, she got lost. Their brains were just not ready for that abstract, worksheet math. The reverse is true, also. Equations she could work on paper did not crossover into real life. Butterfly complained of this. She said to me, "Give me one of those math-problem-of-the-day things. That's easier. Don't give me anymore worksheets. Those are hard and confusing." Mouse, just like his brother, refuses to do worksheet math. However, he knows how to do long division *in his head*.

What does unschooling math look like on a day-to-day basis? Adding and subtracting whole numbers and decimals is practically everywhere, and I think you can probably come up with lots of examples using money, games, sports, and more. The best examples of adding, subtracting, multiplying, and dividing fractions involve recipes and food preparation, maybe also carpentry. Other uses would include scale models, scale drawings, and map scales. Great ways to learn about probability and statistics are through sports and through advertisement claims. These also can be great tools for learning about percent and averages. Sales tax and banking are other opportunities for learning about decimals, besides shopping and earning an allowance. Sewing, carpentry, small-scale architecture and engineering, and art and sculpture are great ways to learn about measurement of lengths and shapes. Square roots, exponents, and negative numbers are all seen primarily in science texts and can sometimes best be explained as to their usefulness within those contexts (distances in space, temperatures, etc.). You can also do what Benezet did and read lots of books that include locations, currencies, and everyday activities that make for good problems to solve.

While many of these examples may not give the appropriate amount of practice that we assume that children need, rote learning may not be necessary if the pleasant experiences of learning with you are cemented in their minds. Learning this way can provide some rich learning experiences full of purpose and meaning but is often more difficult to implement than just giving a child a math textbook. The reward of a child who understands and knows how to use numbers is worth it.

All that being said, I have sometimes had difficulty embracing these concepts, mostly out of fear. I think that is why most homeschooling parents teach math the way the school teaches math. We are afraid that our children will not learn math concepts if we do not make them do it the way we were made to do it. However, my experiences in teaching Tiger arithmetic concepts were a great demonstration of the truth. Most children in school are taught place value and multi-digit addition and subtraction with carrying over in second grade, or age eight. I tried to do the same with Tiger. No matter what I did, she just was not understanding why the numbers had to be in a particular order, why the steps had to be done in a particular order, etc. I stopped teaching it after some frustration on both sides, and when she was about ten years old, it suddenly clicked for her. This happened again and again—with multiplication facts, with long multiplication, and with long division. Because of her repeated frustration with arithmetic, she dislikes math and thinks she is not good at it.

Hawk, on the other hand, has had very little math instruction. He figured out how to skip count by 2, 5, and 10 all by himself. He taught himself to count to 100, values of money, and has his own method of counting up amounts in his head. Anytime I tried to teach him using a book, it was unpleasant and resulted in him temporarily forgetting his own quite accurate methods of figuring. Despite my guilt about not formally teaching him math concepts, he says he likes math and is good at it. As I shared earlier, he aced algebra in 4 months. My two oldest children could be test cases for what happens when you teach math and what happens when life teaches math. Thankfully, I learned my lesson, and Mouse and Butterfly have experienced less math instruction also. We do a lot of problem-solving instead. It has been a long road for me, trying to overcome the brainwashing of so many years of government schooling and the continued well-intentioned, but misinformed, inquiries of relatives.

Writing

Learning to print is largely an imitative endeavor. Many small children will ask you to teach them how to print their names, and then their favorite words. Then, they will begin to write their own little stories with scraggly lines mixed with letters before they write true words. Usually, they do not write true words (unless they ask you how to spell it) until after they have begun to read a bit and know letter sounds and combinations. Having nice handwriting is greatly influenced by fine motor skills development, which is often delayed in boys. All children develop gross motor skills first, and these skills are further refined as the child grows. But fine motor skills take much longer to develop. Charlotte Mason would only require a child to write what she could write perfectly, starting with only one letter or word. If we leave the child alone and teach handwriting as the child asks for it, we would probably avoid a great deal of frustration.

Some things that can help a child develop hand strength and fine motor skills are sculpting with clay, sewing, weaving, and felting. These activities are more enjoyable than making a child use a pencil when he doesn't want to or understand the importance of it.

Writing as an expression of one's ideas also takes time to develop. Many children tell stories long before they can write them down, and even when they have developed the ability to write them down, they often prefer to just tell them orally. Writing requires several skills: planning, organization, large vocabulary, sequencing, understanding of social cues and customs, proper grammar and syntax, and perhaps other skills that I have missed. Some of these are executive function skills that mature over time. Other skills cannot be learned until reading is mastered.

It is very important to accept their efforts without judgement. Too much pickiness about grammar, spelling, and punctuation is discouraging. Another aspect of writing is having something to write about. Children know that people write stories and they write information to share with others. As they grow, they need reassurance that their unique voices are valuable, and they need to be encouraged in their passions so that they are proud to share what they know.

Reading

Reading is probably the one area that causes the most concern among all parents, not just homeschooling parents. Many parents want to get their child reading as early as possible, as if early reading were the single best predictor of future success. However, the Moores inform us in their book *Better Late than Early*, "Some researchers and scholars insist that there is strong evidence that a child's eyes are not physiologically ready for continual and consistent reading until he is at least eight *or even older*. Children's eyes are made primarily for distant vision or for looking at large objects. To require the child to concentrate on near work or upon small objects for any length of time would create undue nervous strain." Isn't it interesting that a child's eyes develop to coordinate with cognitive development? When his brain is ready to learn from the written word, then his eyes are ready, too. And not before. Optometrists regularly tell me that young children become nearsighted because of too much close work at an early age. My own children learned to read fluently at wildly different ages. Tiger learned at age four, Butterfly at age six, Hawk at age twelve, and Mouse is not yet fluent at age ten.

Usually, a child who is between eight and twelve will want to learn to read if he hasn't begun to learn already. In another post on the *Freedom to Learn* blog, dated February 24, 2010, Dr. Gray says that when children are not pressured to read on a timetable, but are free to educate themselves (i.e. unschooled), they begin their first real reading at a remarkably wide range of ages—from as young as age four to as old as age fourteen. Some students learn very quickly, going from apparently complete non-reading to fluent reading in a matter of weeks; others learn much more slowly. Some children can be motivated to read as a means to an end. A few learn in a conscious manner, systematically working on phonics and asking for help along the way. Others just "picked it up." Not all children learn to read on their own, although many will.

One principle noted by many proponents of self-education and which was discussed in the chapter on motivation is that pushing a child to read (or do any skill before he is ready) can backfire. As long as your home is rich in print media, you are reading to them a lot, they are enthusiastic about learning to read, and you are open to feedback from your child about what works best for them, you are on the right track. There is no one *right* way to learn to read, even if you suspect your child is dyslexic.

What does unschooling of language and communication skills look like? This is quite easy to implement. Pen pals, student-run newspapers, journaling, letters to grandma, national magazines accepting writing by children, and creating their own booklets of favorite poems, quotes, and literature passages are all great ways to encourage children to write. Let them dictate their stories to you. Since writing is an extension of speaking as a communication skill, opportunities to speak in front of people, such as 4-H or oral storytelling, can provide other possibilities.

I heard of a great idea called the traveling notebook whereby the parent writes a few sentences or asks questions and leaves the notebook on the child's bed to answer the questions and leave a few sentences or questions of his own for the parent to read and answer. It goes back and forth like that. These are not schoolish questions but rather questions like "How did you like the play we saw?" "What is your favorite movie and why?"

Read great literature to them. Discuss the plot, conflict, emotions, and other elements. Ask them to tell you about the book. What stuck with them and why? Read newspapers. Teach them how to use the library and how to do research of their own. Language is everywhere.

Experiential Learning

Even though children have greater ability to learn from words instead of objects and experiences alone, they still cannot think abstractly. Now they have the capacity to understand the meaning behind holidays and traditions, but their world is still egocentric. They have difficulty imagining other cultural traditions without having at least seen them in a book or on television.

In their book *I Saw the Angel in the Marble*, homeschooling pioneers Chris and Ellen Davis include several essays. In their essay "Whatever Happened to Curiosity?", they say that from birth to about age twelve your child's learning experiences should be as experiential as possible. They strongly recommend creating a rich learning environment in our homes that supports our goals, vision, and purpose for our children. Oliver DeMille writes in *A Thomas Jefferson Education* that during this phase, dubbed "Love of Learning," a child will "play at projects and skills which builds his repertoire of understanding and prowess... The Love of Learner is ripe for exposure to the many areas of human knowledge, with a focus on that which he can experience on his level."

Charlotte Mason said that the mind needs ideas as much as the stomach needs food. In her 20 principles, she said, "In devising a curriculum, we provide a vast amount of ideas to ensure that the mind has enough brain food, knowledge about a variety of things to prevent boredom, and subjects are taught with high-quality literary language since that is what a child's attention responds to best." What are some ways in which we can expose our growing children to a wide variety of experiences, knowledge, stories, and people that are developmentally appropriate?

Experiencing science, history, and geography is probably the most enjoyable aspect of this age group in an unschooling atmosphere. Life science comes alive when you raise and keep different types of creatures, go on nature walks, and visit nature centers. Lots of contact with the natural world makes it easy to see differences and similarities, learn nomenclature and classification, and other basics. Set a good example. Don't be afraid to touch animals yourself. Learn how to display their finds. Give kids the time, the tools, and the opportunity to explore God's creation, and they will learn lots of life science.

In our home, we have raised frogs, fish, triops, hamsters, mice, rats, cats, guinea pigs, darkling beetles, butterflies, and ladybugs and tried to help baby birds. We have also dissected a frog, rat, fish, starfish, crayfish, cow eye, owl pellet, worm, and sheep heart. I know that sounds gross. Notice there are no snakes anywhere in that list. I personally hate snakes and grew up fearing them. However, I did not want my children to be afraid of them. So, when we went to a nature center that had an opportunity to touch and hold a non-poisonous snake, who do you think went first? When we went fishing and my son caught a fish but wouldn't touch it, who do you think had to take the fish off the line? Who volunteered to hold the pet tarantula all the while fearing the possibility of being bitten?

Earth science can be just as relevant. By teaching your children the habit of keen observation and attention, you can help them discover how clouds and wind affect weather; differences/similarities between rocks, sand, and dirt; how rivers and lakes form; the forces that create caves, volcanoes, earthquakes, mountains, tsunamis, and hurricanes; different types of rocks and minerals; and how erosion occurs. Sandbox play, exploring rivers and caves, charting the weather, watching the weather around the world, building models, collecting rocks, and conducting experiments can all give a child experiences with earth science.

One of Mouse's enduring passions is rock collecting. To him, rocks are treasure because they are often shiny and have streaks of color through them. He also uses them in his pretend play with his stuffed animal mice. His interest in rocks led him to learning about gems and mining, coin collecting, and lapidary art. His storytelling and artwork incorporates all that he has learned into elaborate and detailed renderings.

Some of our favorite vacations have been to caves. The wonder of how caves are formed, the unique formations, how they were discovered and used, the stories around them—all of this is fodder for imagination. Often, the kids came home and created their own cave-like dwellings for themselves or their stuffed animal friends.

Physical science can be explored through kitchen chemistry and cooking; a set of magnets; building projects; and a variety of experiments, observations, models, and projects. All of our real-life explorations in this realm have helped our children confront false beliefs. One of the neighborhood kids of about the same age once said, "If we make a pile of magnets large enough, we can make the earth tilt." One of my children replied, "No, you can't. The earth *is* a magnet." They encountered other myths and responded with similar logical answers because of their experiential knowledge, sometimes spoiling the fun.

Mouse attended a science magic show that included a demonstration of how mirrors are used in magic. He immediately wanted to construct a magic box and then became preoccupied with puzzle boxes. He made several of both and took delight in fooling people with his specialized knowledge. I took delight in the fact that he made the experience his own and enjoyed sharing it with others.

History comes to life through biographies and living books, museums, dress-up, games, crafts, and projects. As children learn about earth and life science, it's natural for them to also learn some geography. They can learn additional geography through games and activities. One way we had fun with this was when I created a large 3-D map of the United States using clay. I printed out a topographical map and pasted it to a foamboard. Then, we used different colors of clay to represent rivers and land, piling it up to show mountains. Tiger and Hawk learned states and capitals through a game show hosted by my puppet, Eunice the Unicorn, complete with snarky attitude and funny voice. Butterfly sewed dolls of different skin tones, and we bought fabric scraps so she could make cultural costumes representing different countries around the world. Eventually, she wanted to subscribe to a monthly geography kit that came in the mail. That can be a fun alternative, too. Mouse just likes to curl up with me and read. It doesn't have to be elaborate or expensive.

Just as with younger children, whole experiences are best. All of life is inter-related and interdependent. History is not separate from science or geography. Science, technology, and art overlap in a myriad of ways. Math and language arts are not subjects, but skills used in all areas of life. If we put all the separate areas of study back together again and live with our eyes and ears fully open to life, there are so many opportunities to learn. If schools tell us we need to know all these separate branches of study to function better in the world, then shouldn't the world itself teach us what we need to know of it if we only pay attention? Our culture has successfully analyzed some of the compartments of education. The challenge is now to synthesize that information into a new pedagogy. This new process of educating children is but a rediscovery of what our forebears knew for ages. Nothing teaches quite so well as real experiences with the real world.

Sometimes, computer games and videos can be used to provide a context for learning or create an interest in something. *Finding Nemo* can be used to create an interest in the ocean, fish, or Australia. *Mulan* can be used to create an interest in ancient China. You get the picture. Conversely, you could be reading about ancient China and decide to watch the movie in the context of the book. This provides a springboard for discussing how accurate the movie is and also topics for further exploration.

Inspiration doesn't have to come from visiting places, watching movies, and reading books. Sometimes *you* are the greatest inspiration for a topic of study. Just you being interested in something other than being mom. Living your life in front of your children is the best food for those little people who want so much to be like you (and sometimes become so much like you that you wish you were another person!). After all, most people learn best by imitation. My husband is a history buff, and his favorite topic is World War II. Even though he isn't home all day, guess what? My boys also love history, and one of their favorite topics is, drum roll, please—World War II. We are a family who enjoys cooking and ethnic foods. All but one also enjoys cooking and trying ethnic foods. Because I love nature, I frequently take my children to natural places. Lo and behold, they all appreciate nature. I took a class in Chinese watercolor painting, and even though I didn't enjoy the class, the kids took my supplies and gave it a try. They have endured my interests in fermenting food, including water kefir, kefir, sourdough, vegetables, cheese, and yogurt. They learned a lot about bacteria and digestion this way and experimented with making their own cheeses. All of this is to say that you need to have interests, too, and they will also learn from you. Be careful not to brush them aside, telling them that this is "mom's thing," because they want to be part of your world. Invite them in.

Learning Deeply

I hope that you don't get the impression that you need to be driving around to museums and nature centers, going on educational vacations, buying lots of books and kits, and attending class yourself in order to pursue this lifestyle. Kids of this age group do need exposure to new and varied experiences, but they still need time to digest them. Sometimes, they may even resist your efforts. Don't be afraid to plan activities, but be prepared for them to say no sometimes.

Tiger always loved to go places and complained if too many days went by when we didn't go anywhere, especially as she got older and lost interest in playing. Mouse is the opposite. As I mentioned before, he got really squirrely in the car. Even now, if there are too many stops on a car ride or too many trips in a week, he gets grumpy. But, even he sometimes says, "We don't go anywhere. Can we go somewhere?" Tiger loves museums, but Mouse is happy if I take him to Costco where he gets to eat samples. All kidding aside, he prefers natural settings where he can climb and hide under bushes.

I think the root of it is boredom. They want my creative input because they recognize that mom brings them fresh ideas, although the integration of those ideas into the map of their own minds is up to them. I think that, too, after they have played the same pretend games repeatedly (although with slight variations each time), they pour the passionate energy of those inner thoughts into their world, and thus spent, they need to be refilled with a new passion.

With their lack of knowledge and experience, they cannot necessarily refill their stores without an adult introducing to them a novel idea, experience, person, or other possible interest. So, this dance is a tricky one. We are very much an integral part of the learning process and need to provide discipline and guidance, but we are also the bearers of creative wisdom. Without us, children's knowledge and experience of the world will be limited, but we must be careful to entice them with ideas, not proselytize.

However, sometimes when we are "strewing the path," it can seem like the children aren't interested in anything we are trying to entice them with. It can seem like they don't really do anything new and don't seem to dig deep into anything. They are like butterflies that flit from flower to flower in the same garden. Maybe they don't seem to do anything new because they are digging deeper into things they have been exposed to. Maybe they are trying to explore those things in new ways or revisit old ways because they didn't quite understand it the last time or may have missed something, or are trying to find a new angle. Maybe they don't seem to dig deep into anything initially because they are afraid that mom will make them do work. Maybe they are deep, slow-living type of kids who, while they like new things, also need time to digest them, as I was talking about above. Bombarding them with something new every day may not ensure that they are learning new things, but rather they are not learning anything very deeply and that some things simply aren't truly learned at all. There is not enough time to let it seep into their hearts and souls before the next thing is added. Think of how you feel after going to a homeschool conference. I am usually reeling from all the new information that I have heard and need to take several days just to sort through it all. For them, the experience is probably a bit magnified because they are so young.

The idea that "Well, Butterfly already knows all that stuff and so what *new* things can I teach her" is probably a false assumption. She knows bits and pieces of a lot of different topics, but there is a great deal that she doesn't know about those same topics. There is always something new to learn about even the most basic things. There are new things I can teach her, but allowing her—even encouraging her by way of boredom—to further explore something she already knows a little about can have a broader and deeper impact on her.

I think that is the greatest problem with curriculum. Many do not allow a child to dig deep. In fact, many inadvertently discourage it by scheduling too many books, too many activities, and just plain too much. They only cover material in a cursory manner, such as the entire history of the United States in one year, on top of learning about several areas of science. How can a child know a time period intimately and deeply with such a schedule? Is it more important to try to cram as much information as possible into a child, or is it more important that a child really deeply knows people, places, and events, including God's Creation?

Hindrances

It has been hard for me to grasp that learning and living deeply is not something that happens in a bullet train. It happens on a lazy bike ride through the country. Harder still for me to learn is that for children, everything is in slow motion because so much of life is still fresh and new. It is new for them, but not for me. I want to rush ahead, but they need to linger. I am impatient to move on, but sometimes I need to slow down. Other times, I am the one who remains while they have raced on ahead.

One day, my children came rushing in to show me their latest find: a pillbug. I have seen many, many pillbugs, and their secrets have long lost their appeal for me, but for them, this was only about the third one they'd actually held in their hands. For them, it was almost magical how the little bug rolls itself into a ball and later unrolls itself. *How does it do that? Why does it do that? How do they have babies? What do they eat?* And the next day, *what are those little black specks in there, Mommy?* I did not know the answers to any of these questions (and they don't always want the answers to all of their questions), but I have ceased caring about not knowing the answers, and this bothered me. Have I lived in the world so long that I am no longer awed by Creation? Have I ceased to wonder?

I must become a student of my children and not become so calloused that I cannot appreciate the miracle of even one small pillbug. The greatest minds in history have been inspired by such and never ceased to be amazed. Life is like a smorgasbord of little delicacies waiting to be sampled… and then sampled again. Tickle your taste buds with many delights, but chew slowly. Savor each bite, and don't be afraid to discover a new favorite even as you enjoy old ones. Recline at the table, and prepare to be there a long while, dining with friends.

Another hindrance is a tendency to compare my children or their schooling to another family. Nothing can poison my home more than this comparing. I have often found myself worrying about what other people think about my kids, rather than what God thinks about my kids. I hear what other families are doing or have done and I think, "Wow, that's cool. I want our family to do that." You know, the family that composes a four-part concerto and each plays an instrument. How about the family that builds a Rube Goldberg machine in their backyard or the son who invents and builds his own robot car? What about the girl who knows Latin, Greek, and French? I have visions of children all sitting around the kitchen table working on their lapbooks or notebooks, excitedly talking about what they read and what pictures they are going to include in their books. I have visions of being surrounded by my children on the couch while their ears are all perked for what's going to happen next in the family read-aloud time, Swiss Family Robinson.

Instead, when my children were younger, they had an ongoing game of restaurant in which they were the waiters and cooks. Tiger wrote several different menus. She actually wrote some simple musical scores, but they were memorized, not notes on a page. She came up with simple shows, sometimes live, sometimes with little puppets, and Butterfly did the same thing. They did experiment with cooking and with other kitchen chemicals that I put together in a kit, but they never wrote down what they did and did not measure precisely. They were born naturalists; they were always collecting bugs, pinecones, leaves, feathers, interesting rocks, etc. Tiger was an avid reader, though not always of the books I selected for her, and she is an amazing artist. Hawk made objects and sometimes tried to make machines. Sometimes the machines or vehicles actually worked, but after they were made, he forgot about them. I guess it's the process, not the product, that he was interested in. There was metal and wood everywhere. He would participate with Tiger in her shows sometimes. He loved to cook and created his own soup and cake recipes. These were often too salty or too rubbery, but the process was the important thing. As I mentioned before, I struggled with the mess and the randomness of everything. The two of them had elaborate cities set up in the playroom that took over the entire space. Board games were often missing pieces because they never played the games according to the rules. Instead, they took the pieces and used them for their imagined games. Those two were everywhere at once and never sat for anything. Any time I had them sitting, I couldn't go to the bathroom because when I came back, they'd be gone. Butterfly and Mouse were not so haphazard in their play and were quieter, but I still compared them to other children, too. I sometimes wished Tiger and Hawk, especially, were quieter and studious, more careful about details, more like the children I described earlier. Then God, in His wisdom, showed me a valuable lesson through the science bowl competition.

Our team was very studious, knowledgeable, and quick with correct answers. They did very well on the Q & A portion of the bowl. However, when it came to the solar car portion of the competition, these very studious, bookish traits were no longer an asset, but a hindrance. Children who had had more experience in playing around with building projects, taking old radios apart, and experimenting would have been great assets to the team. Hawk watched the whole thing and begged to be a part of the team, but he wasn't old enough. We ended up not participating in the solar car portion because of the lack of someone with hands-on knowledge. This experience showed me the value of what my children do naturally.

In the opening pages of *Play*, Dr. Brown talks about the Cal Tech Jet Propulsion Laboratory's (JPL) engineers. These were the engineers who put men on the moon. When these men began retiring in large numbers, JPL hired the top graduates from top engineering schools. Even though these grads were great with the theory, they didn't have good problem-solving skills, as their retiring counterparts did. Puzzled by this, management began asking questions and what they found was that "those who worked and played with their hands as they were growing up were able to 'see solutions' that those who hadn't worked with their hands could not." (Brown) What appeared to me to be just "playing around," could be the kind of experience that proves to be an asset in the wider world someday. I encourage you to let go of comparisons and see your child the way God sees him.

Sometimes, when it appears our children are just goofing off, they are unknowingly preparing for their life's work. Remember when I said at the beginning of the book that God has works prepared in advance for your child to do and that *He* prepares that child?

Remember my example of how Hawk's early experiences with Legos has given him a foundation in problem-solving and manipulating 3-D objects? Remember what I said about the opportunities that have opened up for him that demand the exact skills that God has been building in him from the beginning?

This brings me to a third hindrance. In addition to the temptation to rush children's development along and to compare them to other children, we tend to think that they aren't learning anything by spending some of their days just playing. I swung from peace and joy to guilt and worry because of this. There were many days that I let the children play, embracing the idea that they needed that creative time more than academics. But then, I felt guilty because I thought that I wasn't a good homeschool mom by letting them play. I worried that someone might quiz them and find them lacking or be suspicious that my ten-year-old rode his bike around the block at eleven o'clock in the morning. At times, I developed a defensive attitude that I wore like a cloak to protect myself from quizzical stares from strangers and other homeschoolers.

Then, I took Hawk with me to hear a missionary speak at a homeschool literature class that Tiger was taking with her friends. Everyone knew that I did not use a curriculum and that Hawk sometimes gave me a hard time. All of the other children were older than he was and had been reading historical literature and following a curriculum.

Several of the kids were looking at their phones while the gentleman was speaking and all of them, while trying to be polite, looked bored.

Hawk was the only one who was actively engaged. His excitement was palpable, and he scowled at those kids who stared at their phones the whole time. He practically leaped out of his chair to ask questions and was the only one who knew the answers to the missionary's inquiries of the group. I almost fell out of my chair. This kid—the kid who played most of the time—was the only knowledgeable one and, possibly, the only one who gained anything from the missionary's presentation. Maybe all those talks with his dad and the big *Weapons* book I bought from the bargain bin left an impression on him after all.

Putting It All Together

Just like in the last chapter, the emphasis needs to be on whole experiences through service, entrepreneurship, and developing your children's interests and passions through life with you. How you organize your days is totally up to you. Below is a summary of what your day might look like if you take suggestions from this chapter and apply them to your home:

Making meals together
Doing service projects and/or visits together
Spending time outdoors
Getting involved in family business
Reading quality literature
Making creative projects together or individually
Spending some quiet time
Having some free time

If you can incorporate these things into your life with your children, your children's skills in math and communication will develop naturally and with confidence. They will develop a sense of confident competence and a broad knowledge base from which they will find direction as they head into young adulthood in their teen years.

Study Questions

1. How can you incorporate service into your homeschool?

2. How can you encourage and develop entrepreneurship in your children?

3. What surprised you the most about unschooling math, reading, and writing?

4. How could you incorporate more natural means of learning these skills into your life?

5. How can you promote experiential learning in your home? What changes do you need to make?

6. What hindrances resonated the most with you? How can you deal with these effectively?

Chapter 5

Giving Teens the Wings to Fly

Before the 1920s, there was no such thing as a teenager. The unique lifestyle and behaviors of this time in a person's life did not appear in force until after 1938, when the US government passed the Fair Labor Standards Act. This act effectively ended the use of child labor in factories. At the same time, compulsory school attendance laws expanded the upper age requirement to sixteen in most states. This joint prohibition of work and mandatory school attendance for young people created the phenomenon of teen culture that we see today. Is it natural for teens to rebel against authority; experiment with sex, drugs, and alcohol; develop their own language, fashion, and other forms of expression; and behave in reckless, immature ways? Why does this happen and can you expect this to happen in your household if you have been doing things God's way?

I find it interesting that the development of modern teen culture coincides with the widespread compulsion of high school. What is it about high school that gives rise to these aberrant behaviors? When young people are stripped of respect, meaning, usefulness, responsibility, and expectations, the response is to create a parallel existence that has its own distorted values, many of which reject the dominant culture. Imagine a bunch of same age adults in a building together all day, forced to listen to older adults drone on about uninteresting, irrelevant topics. They are not allowed to leave the building and have very little control over what topics they listen to. While there, they are not permitted to do anything that the adults outside the building are doing—no working, no marriage, no ownership privileges. Once they finish their time in this building, they still don't know how to do any specialized work that will allow them to function independently. How would you respond?

Instead of expecting teens to become increasingly responsible and more like adults, many people expect teens to be irresponsible and childish. I've seen blog posts on popular parenting sites that say that teens should be expected to make their beds and load the dishwasher! Seriously? As teens, my kids ran the whole house for 2 days while I attended a conference. Remember what I said about chores in Chapter 2. A teenager should be doing everything you do, including cooking, mowing the lawn, fixing things, and going on errands alone. If you expect responsible behavior and set teens up for success, they are more likely to meet your expectations. Most of society has a low opinion of teens and talk to them in ways they would never talk to other adults. How would you respond if you knew people were suspicious of you and were rude to you most of the time? No wonder some teens vandalize property and rebel.

Before the 1920s, teens worked and, all over the world, even today, they work. Boys were apprenticed at age thirteen to a craftsman to learn a trade and girls were usually married off by age sixteen. Whatever schooling they got, was usually about 3 months out of a year until they were perhaps twelve years old. The rest of the time, they worked with their parents in a shop or on a farm. If they were wealthy, they got private tutoring and still learned in close proximity to a knowledgeable adult, if not a parent. This changed, of course, during the Industrial Revolution because children were exploited by factory owners, and parents sent them to work instead of school to increase the family income. Most of the world still gives adult responsibilities to teens. Only westernized cultures delay adulthood.

I am not in favor of child labor or of limiting educational opportunities. I firmly believe that education lifts people out of poverty and opens doors for youth. However, much of what we teach teens has nothing to do with real life, and they know it. How many teens use their knowledge of chemical bonds, trigonometry, or ancient history in their everyday lives? I am in favor of meaningful learning that can be immediately applied to their lives. How about classes in personal finance, the US Constitution and politics with live debates, conflict resolution, informal logic, or entrepreneurship? Why not partner with businesses to set up week-long apprenticeships for students? We will talk about some of these ideas within a homeschool context in this chapter.

If you have been respecting your children's developmental stages up to this point, particularly during the industry stage from the last chapter, your teen will probably not struggle with the same sorts of issues as public-schooled young people. While most people assume that teen angst is a fact of life, you will find that it is not. As each of my children approached the age of thirteen, family, and even strangers, said to me, "Just wait until they're teenagers." I also heard variations of "Oh, thirteen is the worst" and "The teen years are worse than the toddler years." Really? That has not been my experience. In fact, rather than dreading those years with apprehension, I looked forward to seeing who my children would become.

History Bears Witness

Teens are capable of remarkable feats, and history demonstrates that fact. From ancient civilizations to modern times, some of the most amazing accomplishments have teens at their helm. While ancient people expected more from their youth, many teens of today, too, exceed low expectations and show their true ability. Here is a short, and definitely *not* exhaustive, list of some notable teens:

- Alexander the Great founded his first colony at age sixteen.
- Louis Braille invented the Braille system at fifteen.
- In 2014, Malala Yousafzai won the Nobel Peace Prize at seventeen.
- Balamurali Ambati became a doctor at age seventeen.
- Annie Oakley became a champion sharpshooter at age fifteen.
- Bobby Fischer became a chess grand master at age fifteen.
- Nick D'Aloisio made $30 million from selling his app to Yahoo! at age seventeen.
- Wayne Gretzky was a professional hockey player at age seventeen.
- Laura Dekker sailed around the world solo at age fourteen.
- Flynn McGarry had his own pop-up restaurant at age thirteen.
- Suhas Gopinath became the world's youngest CEO at age seventeen.
- Mark Zuckerberg founded Facebook at age nineteen.

Granted, these teens may be extraordinary in their intelligence, their physical prowess, or their ingenuity. They may have an economic or a social advantage because of their parents or cultural standing.

However, these young people, and others like them that I didn't include, are a testament to the possibilities. How many Suhas Gopinaths and how many Laura Dekkers are sitting in chairs, bored and unmotivated, right now?

Many homeschool parents put their sons and daughters in school when they reach high school age. This is like uprooting a tree that you have carefully tended and putting it in your neighbor's yard just before it bears fruit. I encourage you to remember these young people when the temptation hits you. Can your son become the next Flynn McGarry if he is locked inside a building all day, listening to people talk about subjects that have nothing to do with God's plan for his life?

I know this temptation because I felt the same way as Hawk turned twelve. I prayed about him almost daily, because I wondered how I could keep him home for high school if he avoided doing any schoolish lessons. High school is all about discipline, right? It's all about fulfilling credits and producing a transcript, right? I will talk more about transcripts and credits later in the chapter. I had to expand my view of what high school could be, just as I had with elementary school. God worked in Hawk, too, and brought him to a saving relationship with Himself. When my son made Jesus his Savior, it transformed our relationship too. Praying for your children's salvation should always be your number one priority.

But my expectations of Hawk remained high. I expected him to behave like a man, not a boy, by the time he was fifteen. He even calls himself a young man. He says, "I am not a child. Don't treat me like one." I have always felt that if a person is capable of producing another person, then s/he is not a child anymore. Children do not bear children. Treating teens like adults raises expectations. In their book *Do Hard Things*, homeschooled twins Alex and Brett Harris talk about a "rebelution" against low expectations. They interned at a state supreme court. They ran a political campaign and hired only teens to do the work.

Their team impressed everyone with their professionalism, their skills, their enthusiasm, and the success of their coordinated efforts. They blew every stereotype out of the water, even their own. Alex and Brett call on every teen to rebel against low expectations by doing hard things.

Finding Their Identity in the Wider World

Remember from Chapter 3 that small children try to initiate their own activities to establish a sense of acceptance that they are their own unique persons, separate from parents? At this stage, teens are grappling with a similar issue. They need to wrestle with their identity in the wider world. If they have successfully navigated through both the initiative stage and the industry stage, they know that they have purpose and that they can accomplish things. At this point, they examine family values, cultural norms and values, issues of faith, and God's direction for their lives. Teens often try on different personas to see what feels most like themselves. They may determine a specific career path as a means of identifying with a particular professional group.

It is important to allow teens this time of exploration and not judge them. Just because they dye their hair blue, wear a lot of makeup, or shave their heads doesn't mean anything, really. When Tiger was thirteen, she decided to dye her hair black and she also wore heavy, black, cat eye makeup. She cut one leg off of many pairs of jeans and only wore plaid tops. Her grandmother told her that it all looked hideous. I tried not to say anything. Secretly, I worried. I knew a lot of punks in college, and she adopted a rather punk appearance. She also listened to *screamo* music, cut her hair, and begged for me to let her get a lip piercing. I encouraged her to wait until she was eighteen, that it might maim her face, that she might regret that choice. Two years later, she wanted her blond hair back and started dressing ultra-feminine. Her musical taste skewed more toward pop music, too. She thanked me for not letting her get the piercing.

As she interacted with the world more, she grew to dislike questions about her schooling background and the assumptions that people made about homeschoolers. She tired of the stereotypes, and she strove to prove that homeschoolers are no different than anyone else, that children who learn at home are not naïve and ignorant about pop culture. She did this by immersing herself in the culture, instead of embracing her identity in Christ. At one time, she pestered me incessantly about sending her to school. She struggled with this for much of her teen years and lost touch with her own true passions and calling for a time. However, by the time she turned nineteen, she came full circle, embracing her faith anew and grateful for her years of homeschooling.

Sometimes, I wonder what would have happened if I had never sent her to community writing classes or museum workshops. But my experiences with Hawk confirmed for me that her response to others has nothing to do with me.

Hawk is proud to be homeschooled and enjoys talking about the advantages of his education. Unlike his sister, he never wanted to attend school and embraced the opportunities offered to him with enthusiasm. He is comfortable in his own skin, and when he is challenged by others who say that "Blacksmithing is weird. Who does that?" or "You have ten hobbies? How do you have ten hobbies?", he responds with "I don't sit around playing video games all day. I do stuff." Sometimes, I feel that there is a touch of arrogance there, but he never feels the need to prove himself.

Butterfly recently turned thirteen, but I don't see the angst of her older sister. She has a quiet confidence about her. Her friends all appreciate her and her contributions to their organized plans. They get together for baking days and drama practices that they plan. There isn't anything that she is afraid to try, and since she watched her sister's stages, she also knows what she *won't* do. She has not yet encountered the opposition that her older siblings faced. I hope that she has the courage to stand up for who she is.

Young people who do not successfully find their identity face confusion about who they are and what they're about. They have difficulty choosing a career, finding the right group of friends, and getting motivated to do anything, and they often float along for a while, aimless. These are the adults who flounder and sometimes never get their lives together. Sometimes, if we see this happening, we as parents need to remind our children of what gave them joy as children—before the world invaded their minds.

Abstract Thinkers

Finally, children pass out of the stage when they can only learn from pictorial representation and from words. Now, they begin to think and understand abstractly. This is a process, though. Your kid doesn't wake up on his fourteenth birthday suddenly able to think about things that he can't experience. Just as with previous stages, it develops over several years and isn't complete until he is in his early twenties.

That is the catch. Many curriculums and schools assume that a student is ready for algebra and chemistry when she is fourteen or fifteen years old. Because young people still develop at different rates, only some students will be successful at those ages. The rest will struggle and think that they are just no good at math and science. They avoid it and are afraid of it. Personally, I struggled with both of these subjects, and it is a mystery to me how I even got decent grades in these topics when I attended high school. Maybe the teacher graded on a curve, maybe my short-term memory helped me. I hated math and lived in fear that someone would discover that my B-average was a sham. Chemistry baffled me. I could not see all those electron rings in my mind's eye, and thus, I could not learn it. It took a few more years for my brain to mature before these abstract subjects actually made sense to me. This also happened with Tiger.

However, with heightened memory, reasoning and problem-solving skills, and well-honed language skills, people of this age group learn faster and better than ever before. As I said earlier, academic subjects can be learned at any age, but character cannot. Books that used to take weeks to read now take days. Facts that were forgotten after a couple of months are learned with greater clarity and do not need to be repeated. If your children are not burned out on school from premature teaching, they learn what they need to with ease and enthusiasm during this phase.

Tiger lamented that so many of her friends were unavailable to meet for coffee, even for just an hour. She shared with me that one of her friends cried regularly about the school workload expected of her. Even though my daughter accomplished amazing things during her high school years, she never cried about it and, in fact, enjoyed most of it. My daughter took college level art courses, wrote eighty pages of her first book as part of National Novel Writers Month (NaNoWriMo), participated in a design intensive that involved solving a real-world design problem, and she was selected for a theater critic program through the Goodman Theater. She went to the leadership development and government program, Teen Pact, and she read books like *The Elephant and the Tiger: America in Vietnam* by Albert Marrin, *7 Men Who Rule the World from the Grave* by Dave Breese, along with many others. She spent time apprenticing with a veterinarian, witnessing a cat surgery. There were a few things I asked her to do that weren't her choice, but overall, the objective was to equip her for adulthood and citizenship and prepare her for her life's work.

Hawk's high school experience also includes some amazing opportunities. Like Tiger, he faced persecution for being homeschooled, but unlike her, his challenges came mostly from kids at church. Yes, that's right. One boy said that homeschooled kids don't know anything, that they aren't smart. Another challenged him by subjecting him to "quizzes." When Hawk enrolled in his first college class at age sixteen, he had the last laugh, but he wasn't snotty about it. Like his sister, he also took museum classes and workshops. He gained an introduction to gaming software, 3-D fabrication, television broadcasting, and more. His personal projects include posting YouTube videos about 3-D modeling and creating illustrations for his graphic novel idea. He writes his own songs on guitar and plans to participate in a long-distance bike ride of over a hundred miles. He, too, completes coursework that I requested but that he did not choose. However, before he leaves my home, he will be ready for the challenges that await him.

The keys to successful high school for both were passion and motivation. It goes back to Chapter 2. Intrinsic motivation is powerful, especially at this stage. As young people discover their unique identity, they seek relevance and find a passion to pursue. Usually that passion is related to lifelong interests and skills, but not always. There are many stories of teens who found their passion in high school. The daughter of a friend of mine always loved art and thought she might pursue a career in that. But then, she attended a career fair and saw an architecture exhibit. She became so enamored with it that she decided then and there that she would apply her art skills to that. Last year, she graduated architecture school. You never know what might inspire a young person, so don't stop taking your teen to new and interesting events.

Time to think and explore is still vital. How else will they find their passion? A life stuffed full of classes and extracurriculars leaves little room for inner discovery. Pressuring teens to decide on a career when they may not even have a grip on who they really are often leads to false starts and wasted money later. They need to know that they are accepted and loved *as they are*, not for what they might accomplish. Does your teen know that you will still love him if he chooses not to go to college?

Speaking of College…

There almost seems to be an unspoken code among homeschoolers that, if you homeschool, you have to send your kids to college. Families don't tend to quietly excuse themselves from the group, as if wearing a badge of shame. When it comes to publishing articles about high school, most homeschooling magazines focus on college admissions. Why? Only about 30 percent of jobs require a college degree, and I bet that there are a significant number of included careers that list it as "preferred," not required. For example, many creative jobs might be included in that 30 percent. But, in conversations with professionals, the single greatest factor in hiring is an awesome portfolio, not a degree. As a professional writer, no one asks to see my degree or if I even have one. Clients only want to see who I've done work for in the past and samples of my writing.

Do we pressure ourselves about college because we feel we are held to a higher standard than our public-school counterparts? Do we feel that we are letting down the homeschool movement if our children choose vocational careers instead? Do we fear that our relatives will say, "See! I knew it. She homeschooled those kids, and now they can't get into college. Homeschooling is a recipe for failure."? But, what if God's plan for your child doesn't include college?

Many children raised in Christian homes leave their faith when they live on a college campus for 4 years, even homeschooled children (although their rate of leaving the church *is* lower than the general population of Christians). Is that degree in history worth it spiritually, even though you can tell everyone that she made the honor roll every semester? It is hard to prepare our teens for the possible onslaught of attacks on their faith. Their grades and their scholarship money may hinge on how they respond to this persecution. Is your teen strong enough to stand firm, even when he is threatened with losing that piece of paper so vital to his career choice?

Let's talk about the cost of college. Some homeschooled youth receive scholarship money for college, but many others don't. This latter group is forced to seek federal and private loans, partial grants, parent savings and retirement funds, and even part-time work to subsidize their education. The average 2016 grad carried more than $37K of college debt. At an interest rate of 3 percent over 10 years, the monthly payment for that debt would be a little over $350 a month.

The average starting salary of a student graduating with a communications degree in 2016 was $47K. This means that, when debt is factored in, yearly income was really more like $43K or less, depending on the interest rate of the loan. That was still better than the national average of $35K (unless your degree was in education, which yielded a starting salary of just $35K), however, not as good as a journeyman electrician who, unlike the college graduate, spent the last 4 years as a paid apprentice. That means that he has earned on average around $120K at the same time that a college student racked up $37K *in debt*. And, at the same time that the college graduate gets her $47K, his salary will go up to over $50K or even higher.

We often encourage our sons and daughters to earn a college degree because of perceived financial benefits, even in spite of the debt, as though income is the only measure of success. Looking at my example above, it would seem to me that the young man who did *not* go to college actually has the advantage. After 4 years, he has no debt, could have enough money saved up to buy a condominium or small house, and makes more money than a college graduate. Not only that, he will be able to go home promptly at five o'clock each night, unlike his white-collar counterpart who works overtime without getting paid for it. The extra time with family, friends, and God is far more valuable than the cultural prestige of a college education.

If your child genuinely needs a college degree, please don't prevent him from getting it. I am not discouraging anyone from the education that they need. If your teen wishes to pursue a career in medicine, law, engineering, education, architecture, or any other certifying or licensing field, college is their only choice. Please don't misunderstand me. I am simply noting that many people hang all their hopes on college and don't consider that there are other honorable ways to make a living and support a family. Don't forget that colleges are businesses trying to convince the public that it needs their services. Do your due diligence and ask professionals in the field some questions. What are they looking for in a candidate? Do they always look for a degree? What about internships, volunteer work, and competency certificates such as Cisco or Adobe?

The landscape of work is more competitive than ever before, and many office-type jobs can be outsourced to cheaper options overseas. Some jobs can never be outsourced. They may not be glamorous, but they will always be needed.

Affording College

Even if your son or daughter does need to go to college, don't assume that living on campus for 4 years is the only option available. There are at least three ways to cut the cost of college so the burden of debt is far below the national average. These are the three ways: credit by exam, better known as CLEP tests offered by the College Board, who also administers the SAT and the ACT exams; junior college, which are state colleges that offer all general education credits at a fraction of the cost of a full college or university; and Lumerit Scholar, which is an education technology company with 20 years of experience helping students complete a degree faster and more affordably. Let's talk more about each of these options before I talk about alternatives to college.

According to their website, the College Board has offered credit by exam for more than 40 years. Credits earned this way are accepted by nearly three thousand colleges and universities. Your student can use one of the Board's study guides to prepare for any of the thirty-three exams they offer, and each exam only costs about $80. The tests are administered in more than eighteen hundred test centers nationwide, including local junior colleges. Your student can even start getting college credit this way while still in high school. Imagine how much money you could save if your teen earned at least some of his college credits this way. Check out their website to see how it works and what tests are offered.

Attending a local junior college can also be a good option, and very often, they will allow your teen to start while still in high school if you are homeschooling. Just like any other college, they do offer financial aid and limited scholarships. Scholarships usually require full-time attendance and a graduation plan, as well as decent grades in high school. Some are small, department awards. However, because of the lower cost, your teen might not need aid since he will spend $8K–$10K on 2 years of college instead of nearly $40K for a public university or $66K for a private one during the same time period, on average. Another advantage of junior college is that, if your student is a bit shy about large classrooms, he can ease into higher education with their smaller class sizes. He can also continue to live at home, cutting room and board costs, and reducing the opportunities for secular influence. The downside is that junior college classes are often not as challenging and transfer students have less scholarship opportunities. However, some states have partnership agreements set up between junior colleges and participating state and private universities whereby credits accumulated at the junior college are guaranteed to transfer. In Illinois, it is called the Illinois Articulation Initiative. Check out the website for the Education Commission of the States to find out more about your state's program.

Lumerit Scholar has a unique program that has evolved over the past 20 years. For a set monthly fee, your student can complete nine or more courses in a year. Nine courses are about the same as she'd do at a junior college, but Lumerit allows her to complete those courses for about half the cost. They also guarantee that all the courses will transfer to the college of her choice. Everything is done online, so your student can work and live at home while gaining college credit. Your student can even start while still in high school. Check their website for more details. (I will note here that I *do not receive any commission* for mentioning their program or any other program in this book.)

Before I move on to college alternatives, I have one last point. If your teen was not very studious or life circumstances led to an inability to homeschool high school with confidence (but you still kept her home), take heart. While earning a GED is not ideal, it also doesn't need to be a badge of shame. A GED will allow your teen to go to junior college, and no one will know about her high-school experience. If your child is currently in high school and you are afraid to take him out because you think he won't get an education, take him out. A dear friend of mine had a son who, in high school, caused her much worry because he kept skipping school and hanging out with the wrong crowd. She felt that God was calling her to take him out of school. She feared for his future, but she feared the Lord more and obeyed. She took him to work with her everyday so she could keep an eye on him and so he could learn work ethics. Years later, he thanked her. He was the only one out of his group of friends who didn't get killed or end up in prison. Trust the Lord. He knows the best path for your teenager.

College Alternatives

There are many high-paying jobs in the construction, healthcare, and sales fields that require no more than completion of a 2-year program, and some only require a high school diploma. According to *300 Best Jobs Without a Four-Year Degree* by Dr. Lawrence Shatkin and Michael Farr, these jobs include the following: electrician, plumber, pipefitter, auto mechanic, commercial truck driver, insurance representative, wholesale and manufacturing sales representative, real estate broker, welder, registered nurse, dental hygienist, and radiology technician. These are just a handful of the possibilities. Check out local vocational schools and 2-year programs at junior colleges to see what programs are available to your teen. Another possibility along these lines is an apprenticeship, and some of the jobs listed in *300 Best Jobs* involve a paid apprenticeship as part of the training. Check out another book by the same authors entitled *200 Best Jobs Through Apprenticeships* for more information about this option.

There are two programs that won't be listed in either of these books, though. One is Praxis, and the other is Huge UX School. Both of these are paid apprenticeship programs, but not in traditional fields. Praxis partners with fast growing business start-ups and accepts participants who demonstrate a personality that fits well with their ideology. There are no quantifiable standards that they look for. There is an interview and application process, but they have accepted a diverse cohort of people—from high school dropouts to college graduates. Hawk is very interested in this option because he is not keen on sitting through lectures. He possesses many of the qualities that make him a good match for their program. Generally, if your son or daughter is an independent thinker, highly motivated, entrepreneurial-minded, flexible, and teachable, Praxis might be a good fit. Check out their website for more details. Huge UX School is the education arm of Huge, Inc. This company handles marketing for Fortune 100 businesses. They struggled to find the right caliber talent to work for them so they decided to start a program to train the talent themselves. Each summer, they offer a 10-week, paid apprenticeship with some of their top designers. Competition for this program is fierce and involves some preparation. If your graduate doesn't know how to use the Adobe Creative Suite, don't bother applying for this program. That's where my next college alternative comes in.

Computer training centers offer courses in Adobe software, web development, internet security, and more. Passing competency exams and becoming a certified expert can be unconventional ways to open the door to technology-based careers and can be done while your student is still in high school. Many creative fields expect proficiency in their respective software plus a portfolio demonstrating ability and style. Degree programs teach these same software packages, but for a great deal more money. Couple this with an agency that matches applicants with employers, and your student could be on the fast track. This is the option that Tiger is taking. She was interested in Praxis but did not want to move to a new city, which often happens in their program. Tiger is pursuing the designation of Adobe Certified Expert in three of their software programs, which will also qualify her to become a Design Specialist. She hopes to use her training to get an entry-level position as a graphic designer.

One last alternative to consider is entrepreneurship. Remember this pillar of life of an eight- to twelve-year-old? Remember the story about Hawk and his 3-D printed customized figures at the beginning of the book? Starting his own business is Hawk's ultimate goal. He chooses to dream and to find out how to make that dream a reality. The American economy is founded on small businesses, and the lack of people taking that risk over the past generation contributes to the general lack of business growth and new jobs. Today's young people are more open to taking charge of their futures through owning their own businesses so they can make a difference, engaging in meaningful work. The trend toward self-employment is reflected in the fact that 50 percent of the workforce is expected to be doing some form of freelancing by 2020, according to an article in *Entrepreneur* magazine published May 24, 2016. Many shy away from this option because it seems risky. Putting all your eggs in one basket is risky, too. As a self-employed, professional writer, I will say that it takes a lot of hard work to get a business going.

However, I do not work for just one person, as an employee does. I often have three or more clients, and it is unlikely that all of them will end our relationship at the same time. If your teen is motivated, has a great idea, is teachable, and focused, entrepreneurship might be a good fit. There are many, many good books out there (and websites) that will teach your teen how to run a successful online business or start-up. See the Resources posted on my website for a list of these.

The Importance of Balance

In the chapter about little children, I mentioned the increasing rates of anxiety and depression among children. Then, earlier in this chapter, I mentioned Tiger's friend who cried about the school workload her parents expected her to complete. While stress-related mental disorders can be seen in children as young as six years old, the highest rate of increase is among teens. Some experts estimate that as many as 25 percent of them suffer from anxiety and/or depression. Even though modern young people ought to have less to worry about than those of the Great Depression, the data shows the exact opposite. In the last 80 years, anxiety and depression symptoms have steadily *increased*, not decreased. In fact, the suicide rate among people aged fifteen to nineteen hit its highest rate in 40 years in 2015 at 14.2 deaths per 100,000 youth, according to the Centers for Disease Control and Prevention. It is the second leading cause of death for this age group. Why?

As I mentioned in Chapter 3, one of the key factors is a lack of control over their lives. Homeschooled youth are not immune to feelings of worry, hopelessness, isolation, and worthlessness. I knew a few homeschooled teens who harmed themselves as a means of managing their depression. These girls suffered from low self-esteem, loneliness, and feelings of worthlessness. They were surrounded by their parents and siblings all day, so you wouldn't expect it, but some of these girls had very controlling mothers. The parents fought and eventually divorced.

I knew a few other teens who did not harm themselves but seemed depressed regardless. They either had a heavy workload, or they had little parental support for their ambitions.

Because this is a key time for young people to develop their unique identity, it is imperative that they exert a great deal of control over their destinies at this important juncture. They need to be collaborators in choosing their courses, their extracurriculars, and everything else. Their voices matter, and they need to feel that *they* are charting their course, not you. When we give teens the reins, they grow in self-confidence and self-worth. When we value their input, their ideas, and their feelings, they feel they have important contributions to make. It is one way to protect them from the hopelessness of depression.

Another key factor in the increase of anxiety and depression among teens is loneliness and social isolation. This sounds strange in our connected world, but superficial and artificial social media "friends" and "likes" are not the same as deep, face-to-face, human connections. A teen may have three hundred Facebook friends and only one real friend that she can tell her deepest secrets to. Unfortunately, that friend may live 1000 miles away. With the lack of privacy and trust in our current digital world, it is hard for *anyone* to develop real friendships, let alone teenagers. Contributing to this problem is cyberbullying (yes, that happens to homeschooled teens, too) and too much emphasis on academics, once again. We need to allow time for teens to just have fun together, and homeschool gym doesn't count. Host a game night or a movie night in your home. Invite a local celebrity over for a teen salon. Have a candles-cookies-and-coloring night with adult coloring books and a bunch of teen girls, all sipping hot chocolate. One mom in our group hosted a Flash Friday teen event once a month. Everyone brought a flashlight and did some sort of small service project, such as picking up trash in a park. Then, they all headed over to the church for a retro science fiction movie night with popcorn. Friendships and leisure time are just as important, if not more so, than the coursework. Make it happen.

Charting Your Course

Well, now it's time to start talking about coursework. Most of the time, parents plan high school classes based on college admissions requirements and on their state's high school graduation requirements. I live in Illinois, so I will share what my State Board of Education says about it as of September 2015, and yours is probably similar.

- 4 years of language arts, to include 1 writing-intensive course. The required second writing-intensive course can be fulfilled in another subject area, such as social science
- 3 years of mathematics, one of which must be Algebra 1, with another including geometry content
- 2 years of science
- 2 years of social studies, one of which must be the history of the US or a combo of US history and government, with another semester being civics
- 1 year of one of the following: art, music, foreign language, or vocational studies
- 4 years of physical education
- A half credit of health and a quarter credit of consumer education

All of these classes total only 16.75 credits. The public high school usually adds 3.25 credits of electives to that so that all graduates have 20 credit hours, or four courses plus gym class every year. Colleges generally like to see what I call the "4 x 4"—4 years English, 4 years math, 4 years hard sciences, and 4 years social sciences. They usually like to see at least 2 years of a foreign language as well. Two private schools in my area require 22–24 credits. It is generally accepted that 120 contact hours constitutes 1 high school credit, or Carnegie unit. However, it does not specify whether those hours must be completed using a textbook, video series, group of projects, audiobook, field study, or other means. Also, what happens if your son finishes the textbook in 4 months instead of 1 year? Does that still count as 1 credit? And what if your student is not destined for college?

When I planned high school for my children, I knew that their credits would be completed in an unconventional manner. Since my state classifies home schools as private schools, I could play with the requirements for graduation a little bit to satisfy what I felt they needed. The beauty of homeschooling is the ability to customize each child's education. I took full advantage of this fact. I did not penalize my children for completing typical high school work in less time than what was considered average. To me, it didn't matter how long it took to finish a textbook; it still counted as 1 credit. Tiger took summer intensives through 826CHI, a non-profit writing and tutoring center, that earned her credits in a condensed time period. Two weeks of workshops at 30 hours a week equals a half credit, right? We attended live performances of Shakespeare plays, which I felt were more valuable than simply reading them to each other, even if it took less time. It didn't matter if my son listened to a novel or read it himself; it still counted toward English literature. If the average student read four or five classics in one year, wrote two term papers, and completed comprehension questions, then my students received the same credit even if they read those books in less time. What I'm getting at is that you can give an English credit for writing a book or posting to a blog twice a week; it doesn't have to be a formal program. You can give science credit for assisting a botanist at the Chicago Botanical Gardens or completing a master gardener course with your university extension program. Be creative. Talk with your teen about what he'd like to do to meet his graduation requirements.

I recommend taking a look at two resources, *The Teenage Liberation Handbook* by Grace Llewellyn and *College Without High School* by Blake Boles. Llewellyn's book includes a plethora of ideas for finishing high school strong while still staying true to your teen's passions and interests.

Boles' book questions the whole high-school phenomenon and gives insight into what colleges are actually looking for when they sort through all the applications. He outlines five qualities—intellectual passion, leadership ability, logical reasoning skills, ability to learn in a structured environment, and background knowledge. In his book, he shows teens how to meet these qualities without doing traditional high-school coursework and he shows teens how to jumpstart their college education, if that is their path.

Admissions at highly selective colleges aren't even based on transcripts. Everyone who applies to the top schools has the same profile—awesome test scores, perfect GPA, Advanced Placement (AP) courses, National Honor Society—so how do admissions officers decide? They decide based on who shows signs of being a person of eminence. A person with that type of potential does something extraordinary during his teen years. He starts a successful business. He walks the Appalachian trail or completes a cross-country bike trip. He writes a novel. Basically, he does one or more of the things that I've been talking about in this book. Encourage your teen to do hard things, to dare to dream and take steps to fulfill those dreams, even if he isn't going to college.

If college isn't your child's path, then you can be even more creative since almost no one will ever ask about a transcript. A couple of homeschooled teens I know started taking college classes while in high school and they did not even have to submit a partial transcript. The junior college never did ask for one, and the teens continued to take classes there. When Tiger completed high school at home and applied for retail jobs, only one prospect asked for a copy of her diploma. Our assumption is that our teens must have a transcript, but more than likely, only a college will look at the classes, while everyone else just wants to see a diploma, if anything.

Two Ways to Prepare Transcripts

There are basically two ways to prepare your child's transcript. The first way is the traditional listing of classes with the number of credits earned and the grades listed next to them. This style looks a lot like an Excel document. You can see a couple of examples of this style under Resources at my website, www.juliepolancobooks.com. On the back of this summary spreadsheet, parents usually attach a list of books and other resources they used. Every school has its own format, so don't worry if yours doesn't look like your friend's, but make sure that it looks polished and professional. Do not handwrite it or use notebook paper.

A second way to present your child's high school work is a narrative transcript. This is similar to the portfolio approach described in the Record-Keeping chapter near the end of this book. You do not assign credits or grades; instead, you describe skills and experiences. Here is an example from Tiger's narrative transcript:

Art Studies

Tiger has taken two college level courses with Rebecca George, founder of the community art center, The Art House, and faculty at the School of the Art Institute of Chicago. In one course, Tiger was challenged in her drawing skills and in the other, Tiger had the opportunity to explore different art materials and methods and how they combined with each other to create original works. Tiger also took two courses, Introduction to Digital Art and Graphic Design I, at the local community college, which introduced her to creating digital works using the Adobe Creative Cloud. Later, to help her understand and apply the design process with a real team and a real client, she participated in a summer institute design intensive with Till School, founded by the Huizengas, who are faculty at Columbia College and Northwestern University design departments.

And it goes on from there. A narrative transcript gives a more complete picture of what your son or daughter accomplished during their high school years. However, not everyone will accept this format. I actually prepared both. You can see a more complete example of a narrative transcript at my website.

Celebrating the End of a Journey

Well, your teen did it. She finished the course set out for her. You respected her developmental timetable, you included her in the process, and now, it is the end. Such a worthy accomplishment deserves a celebration. Will it be a blow-out party at a banquet hall or outdoors, in a forest preserve? Will you invite all your friends and family to your house and formally present your son or daughter with a diploma and a few remarks? Will it be a private affair at a fancy restaurant?

For years, my homeschool support group hosted a formal graduation ceremony with a nice reception afterwards. The graduates wore a traditional cap and gown. It included the presentation of diplomas by each family, allowing each one to say a few words about their graduate. A volunteer prepared a slideshow of the graduates, a gift that celebrated their homeschool journey from birth to adulthood. One of the fathers usually gave a short message and a formal reception followed. It was very elegant and designed to present homeschoolers in a positive light to those naysaying extended family members who might attend. My homeschool group grew to more than sixty families, so that made it possible to do such an event. It has now shrunk to half that. It is but one model for celebrating the journey for both parent and child.

Study Questions

1. Examine your expectations of teens. How do they need to change?

2. How can you help your teen find his unique identity? Think of some specific steps unique to your situation.

3. What surprised you most about the sections addressing college? How did this impact you?

4. Has there been imbalance in your teen's life and how can you address this?

5. How can you creatively meet high school requirements and collaborate with your teen?

6. How will you celebrate the end?

Chapter 6

Spreading the Banquet

I n my home, I have different kinds of eaters. If I serve meatloaf, mashed potatoes, and broccoli, this is what happens. Mouse may not eat any of it and ask for a big sippy cup of milk. Butterfly will ask for meatloaf and either eat all of it and then eat her favorite food, apples, or she will pick at it. Hawk will eat meatloaf, a little bit of mashed potatoes with lots of salt, and only eat broccoli if it is raw. Tiger will eat a little of everything, but her stomach may not be full when she pushes her plate away. If I make muffins and bacon for breakfast, Butterfly and Mouse will eat the bacon, but pick at the muffin. Hawk might decide he's sick of bacon and muffins and make his own breakfast. Tiger might eat both, but not continue to eat until she feels full.

When we introduce our children to the wonderful bounty of possibilities past and present, the parade of noble people, creatures, events, and more, we are spreading a banquet of learning before them. However, just as when we serve dinner, each child has a unique way of approaching the banquet.

The Baby The baby is the child who looks at the banquet and prefers his baby food. He may eat little tidbits of especially tasty or simple foods, but mostly he prefers his milk.

The Picky Eater The picky eater is usually a young child who either only eats her favorite food(s) or grazes. She avoids eating certain foods because of taste or texture. This child will sometimes sneak a favorite food or fill up on snacks if she doesn't like what's on the banquet table.

I Want It My Way The My Way eater is an older child who eats most foods as long as they are prepared a certain way. If they are not, he may decide to make it himself. Sometimes he has a taste for something that is not on the banquet table and will make it himself. He is always well fed because of his initiative.

Eat Anything This type of eater is mom's favorite. She eats whatever is put before her, whether it is her favorite or not. If she doesn't like something, she will simply take only a little of it. While this child is a compliant eater, she may sometimes go hungry because she doesn't fill up on foods she doesn't like and won't make her own food.

Diners at the Banquet of Learning

The banquet table is analogous to spreading a banquet of learning. We try to spread a feast of a variety of different people, places, and events in a variety of preparations. These preparations may be books, movies, field trips, tools, kits, classes, and any other presentation we can dream up. The way each child approaches the banquet table of learning depends upon his age, but also his personality. Below are the same types of eaters I already described above, but rephrased according to the way each type learns.

The Baby The baby is the child that is not yet ready for the banquet of learning. If you are sensitive to the child's needs and try simple projects, he may come to the banquet. Otherwise, trust that when he is ready to move from milk to solid food, he will.

The Picky Eater This is a child who is ready for the banquet, but who may become passionate about one topic or who doesn't seem to be really interested in anything. She may decide she will only read books about butterflies or fairies and nothing else. Every movie, every project, is about fairies and butterflies. On the flipside, she may seem to dabble in everything, not really digging too deep into anything. One day, it may be flowers. The next day, it may be the moon. The day after that, it may be ballerinas. She may only read one book about each thing and a storybook at that. The child who is this type of eater/learner may be any age, not just a young child.

For the one who is passionate about only one topic, the strategy is the same as if you were feeding her from your dining table. To encourage the child to try other areas of interest, you must continually present other possibilities. Clothe it in a family trip to a museum or natural place. Leave books from the library in places where your child would see them. Another strategy might be to use their passion as a jumping point to something related. In the example above, fairies and butterflies might segue into flowers that attract butterflies. Encourage her interest and show genuine enjoyment of what she loves to foster trust between you and your child. If she trusts you and you are gentle and non-pressuring in presenting related areas of possible interest, she may be willing to try something a little new. I would caution you not to discourage a passionate interest; it may become a lifelong passion that directs the child's path as she grows older. If it does not, she becomes an expert in something that she cares about.

For the grazing version of the Picky Eater, the approach is only slightly different as with the single passion version. If your child only dabbles in ideas but none take hold, be encouraged that at least she has been exposed to it. She will more than likely become interested in some of those ideas again. Like the grazing eater who takes bites of things that look good and then matures into a true diner, the grazing learner will also mature into a true participant in the banquet of learning. Continue to allow her to choose from among several choices of books you have brought home from the library. Continue to take her to places that she and you would enjoy. Continue to talk with her about projects you can do together.

I Want It My Way This type of learner wants to plan the banquet himself. He doesn't mind if someone helps him as long as it is done to his specifications. He may be the type that doesn't mind if you plan to expose him to the Civil War, but it better be a live re-enactment or documentary series, not a craft or book. If you don't pay attention to the way that he likes things presented, he may decide that a topic is boring or that you don't know what you're talking about before you even get a chance to put it on the banquet table. Think about the child who has only had canned asparagus and so he decides that he hates asparagus. Then he has fresh asparagus in a restaurant one day and his whole world is turned upside down because he has discovered that he loves asparagus. In much the same way, the My Way learner can develop attitudes about certain ideas because of the way they are presented. A corollary to this possibility is that the My Way learner also has a tendency to think that he knows all about something after minimal exposure (also like the asparagus example). He might go to a Civil War re-enactment and come away not with an interest in learning more, but with a false confidence that he now knows all about the Civil War.

On the one hand, unschooling this type of child can be very easy because he naturally wants to plan the banquet of learning himself. He does not need coaxing. However, if left entirely to himself, the child might become arrogant and intolerably proud. He needs a loving parent to show him what he doesn't know by wisely and gently raising the bar. He, too, needs to be exposed to a variety of ideas, but unlike the Picky Eater, he needs to have more complex and richer dishes as part of his banquet to show him that he doesn't know all about rice after eating only white rice. He needs each idea to be presented in a lively, interesting way (but not necessarily entertaining) to prevent him from developing prejudices against ideas. When he doesn't know what to put on his banquet and is confronted with his own ignorance, the parent who has established a pattern of offering to prepare some items for his banquet might find her services requested at his dining table, even if grudgingly.

Eat Anything This is not only mom's favorite type of eater, but is also mom's favorite type of learner. This learner will do almost whatever you ask. Unlike the My Way learner, the Eat Anything learner is not particularly motivated to plan her own banquet of learning. She may sometimes slip into a grazer mode, but she is not really picky about what she learns or even if she learns. She will wait for mom to serve up the next idea and tell her when to do something with the idea rather than go and teach herself something. She will eat whatever is served most of the time, but don't ask her to do more than the minimum if it's something she doesn't particularly like. If mom doesn't present the ideas, the child may not pick up any books, except to graze.

This child has lost some of her natural initiative and may even suffer a bit from learned helplessness. Sometimes a child just doesn't want to put forth the effort to teach herself or she is afraid of failure. Whatever the reason, at some point, mom has to gradually give the charge of the kitchen over to the child or the child will never learn how to prepare a meal for herself. It is important to partner with the child in every way possible—choosing topics or ideas to investigate, choosing materials to use, choosing how deep or how shallow to go with the topic, choosing projects to do, etc. just as you would if you were teaching a child to cook. Over time, the child should be doing more and more of these organization and planning skills herself. This child needs to develop empowerment, initiative, and a sense of competence. This type of learner is the hardest to unschool because the child has difficulty making choices and would rather go hungry for knowledge than have to find her way among all the possibilities. She needs help narrowing those choices. A small banquet that gradually gets larger or has some dishes removed is most manageable for this type of learner.

As we seek to spread a banquet of learning possibilities before our children and invite them to come and taste, we can do only that—invite them to taste. We cannot force them to eat or the food will lose its flavor. Understanding what type of learner(s) we have in our homes is important to understanding how to spread the banquet for them. That is what we are doing. We are lovingly preparing a feast for them to experience and remember for a lifetime. Our legacy will be their ability to spread their own feasts for themselves and others.

Study Questions

1. What type of learner(s) do you have in your home?

2. What changes to your style of teaching or strewing the path do you need to make to reach your child(ren)?

3. What is your own style of learning? How does your style of learning challenge or impact you in your ability to reach your children?

Chapter 7

Getting Started

In the last chapter, we explored the idea that your home may have different types of learners and we discussed some ways that you might handle each type of learner. After reading this book, you are probably wondering, "Okay, all this sounds great, but what does it look like on a practical level? I mean, how do I get started on this natural learning, unschooling lifestyle?"

That question plagued me for quite a while, to be honest. I was very confused about what my role was and kept slipping back into using a planned curriculum for some subjects. In the end, those, too, felt unnatural even if I had asked my children if they'd like to learn about the subject matter and described the curriculum to them. It felt like a security net for me because then I'd have something that I could write down for the records I was keeping and I'd have something to tell the relatives. I felt like we were *doing something*, but then I'd see Hawk curled up in a chair with my husband, talking and reading about World War II aircraft or I'd notice Tiger reading *Voice of the Martyrs* or *God's World News* magazine. I would think to myself, "Why am I spending money on a history curriculum?"

The first thing to do is pray. Pray fervently, and ask God what He wants you to do. As I described at the beginning of this book, I felt like I was at the end of my rope and I had to humble myself and ask God to take control of our homeschool in a very literal sense. Ask Him to forgive you for wrong attitudes and behaviors. Ask Him to speak truth into your heart. Ask Him what His desires are for your family. Keep a notebook handy.

Throw out curriculum catalogs, homeschool magazines, and related publications. For me, these items tend to keep me enslaved to a school mentality. There can be useful articles in them about encouragement, parenting issues, record keeping, etc., but truly, we must first look to Scripture and prayer for most of these issues. Most of the advertising and articles in these publications promote a school-at-home lifestyle, feelings of inadequacy, inappropriate worship of achievement, and simply frustrated efforts to be free from those encumbrances. Keep articles that are useful, but throw the rest out. You will not need curriculum catalogs. No one outside of a school uses curriculum. You will be using great literature, museums, natural places, vacations, newspapers, and other real-life resources. If you feel in need of a math or reading curriculum at some point, you can read reviews and purchase it used or borrow it from a friend.

I know it can be hard to throw this stuff away. It was for me. As I mentioned earlier in this book, I am a sucker for glamorous advertising. I was afraid I'd be missing out on something. But then I realized that this was an idol for me. Throwing everything out was an act of faith. It was like I was saying to God, "I do believe you. I do want you to lead this homeschool. I will rely on you and your Word only, for guidance. I will fully embrace life without these crutches."

Play with your children, if you don't already. If your life has been filled with schedules and curriculum, this may be the first time you have actually played with your children in a long time. Offer to play a board game. Take them to the park, and play chase games or go swing on the swings with them. Go skating with them. Make some puppets together, and put on a little show (or you make puppets and they watch your show). Don't make this an "educational" time. Do not attempt to make it a "teachable moment." The point here is to have fun with them, show them they can trust you to be with them and not make them do stuff, renew your relationship with them, show them you value who they are. This needs to be non-judgmental, non-directed playtime together.

Forget about whether you are "wasting" time or what you are *supposed* to be doing. I'm not suggesting that you forget about washing dishes, doing laundry, or cooking, but don't let a little dirt or dust keep you from playing with your children. This is vital time with them that you will never be able to recapture. If tomorrow you discovered your son or daughter had a terminal illness, how do you want to remember your time together?

Find likeminded friends. This may be hard, depending on where you live. You may only be able to find likeminded individuals on the world wide web. No matter where you find them, though, it is very important to have at least one other Christian friend who shares your educational philosophy and values so that you can encourage each other, support each other, bounce ideas off of each other, and sometimes even gently rebuke each other. It is hard enough to homeschool in a vacuum. It is harder still to follow the path of natural, Christ-led, learning in the face of a continual shift toward curriculum-driven homeschooling, especially among Christians.

Live a full life. This concept has been the most difficult for me to grasp. What does this mean? Well, different people have different ideas about what this means, but the Bible is the first place to look for how to live our lives and Proverbs 31:10-31 is generally held to be the standard of feminine excellence:

"(13) She seeks out wool and flax and works with willing hands to develop it. She is like the merchant ships loaded with foodstuffs; she brings her household's food from a far country. She rises while it is yet night and gets spiritual food for her household and assigns her maids their tasks. She considers a new field before she buys or accepts it, expanding prudently and not courting neglect of her present duties by assuming other duties; with her savings of time and strength she plants fruitful vines in her vineyard. She girds herself with strength—spiritual, mental, and physical fitness--for her God-given task and makes her arms strong and firm. She tastes and sees that her gain from work with and for God is good; her lamp goes not out, but it burns on continually through the night of trouble, privation, or sorrow, warning away fear, doubt, and distrust. She lays her hands to the spindle, and her hands hold the distaff. She opens her hand to the poor. Yes, she reaches out her filled hands to the needy, whether in body, mind, or spirit. (26) She opens her mouth in skillful and Godly Wisdom, and on her tongue is the law of kindness (giving counsel and instruction.) She looks well to how things go in her household, and the bread of idleness—gossip, discontent, and self-pity—she will not eat. Her children rise up and call her blessed (happy, fortunate, and to be envied); and her husband boasts of and praises her, saying 'Many daughters have done virtuously, nobly, and well with the strength of character that is steadfast in goodness, but you excel them all. Charm and grace are deceptive, and beauty is vain because it is not lasting, but a woman who reverently and worshipfully fears the Lord, she shall be praised." (30) (Amplified)

Living a full life means that we are not spending our days in idleness. We are also walking in the Holy Spirit, day and night. We are seeing to the needs of our families and to the needs of others. We are to "live purposefully and worthily and accurately, not as the unwise and witless, but as wise (sensible, intelligent people), making the very most of the time, buying up each opportunity, because the days are evil." (Ephesians 5:15, Amplified). Paul writes just before this verse that we are to "try to learn in your experience what is pleasing to the Lord (let your lives be constant proofs of what is most acceptable to Him). Take no part in and have no fellowship with the fruitless deeds and enterprises of darkness, but instead let your lives be so in contrast as to expose and reprove and convict them." (Ephesians 5:10-11, Amplified).

How do we decide what is worth doing, reading, listening to, etc.? I tend to use Philippians 4:8 as a guide: "Finally, brothers, whatever is true, whatever is noble, whatever is right, whatever is pure, whatever is lovely, whatever is admirable—if anything is excellent or praiseworthy— think about such things." Living a full life will look different for each family, for each person, as God directs. However, the common themes are directed by the Holy Spirit—serving our family, other believers, and those in need; living purposefully to please God; and not engaging in fruitless activities that lead us away from God. As Paul wrote in 1 Corinthians 6:12: "Everything is permissible for me—but not everything is beneficial." We need to focus on those activities that are beneficial to our families and others. As discussed in the chapters about each age group, service, entrepreneurship, play, time outdoors, and time spent in meaningful projects and books are great ways to spend our time in Godly pursuits.

Instruct your children through relationship. If you get nothing else out of this book, I hope that you get the message that God meant for us to educate our children through our relationship with them. The closer your relationship is, the easier it is to discipline, to teach, to rebuke, to guide. We develop relationship not by being dictators, nor do we help them by being doormats. We develop relationship with our children by walking with them day by day, just as our relationship with our Heavenly Father grows by steadily walking with Him day by day.

We talk with them, we do things with them, and we model for them. Our relationships are meant to be intimate, just as God knows us intimately. This is the only way that we can be effective in reaching our children's hearts and minds for Christ. It is the only way we can accurately assist in developing our children's natural bents. This is not necessarily easy to do, especially if you have had a rough road with one or more of your children, but it can be done and is well worth it. Start with just playing with them, as mentioned above.

Our role is to make life sparkly. It is not enough to just let your child do what interests him. You should know him so intimately that you can entice him, inspire him, draw him in with what you present because *it speaks to his heart.* You have laid before him the very books, magazines, trips, projects, whatever, that he has been longing for and didn't know it, and you have only been able to do that because of your relationship. God is so jealous for relationship with us that he paid the highest price. Our relationship with our children is meant to model our relationship with Christ. We, too, are asked to pay the highest price.

I did not begin to experience the true joy that God had for me until I was able to fully embrace the incredible blessing that the relationship with Him is. He revealed to me a wall of anger, fear, and resentment that was keeping me from the ecstatic, boundless love that He has for me.

Without that, I could never experience joy in my circumstance of being home with four young children. I could never invest in my relationships with them.

On a practical, day-to-day level, just do stuff! Your whole day is open to you if you are not enslaved to a curriculum or worldly standards. In previous chapters, I mentioned being organized and having a rough plan. Even if you are leading an unschooled life, planning can help you accomplish all that you and your family desire.

My family recently went on a trip to Florida. We had several goals in mind. We wanted to see my grandmother and my husband's cousin while we were there. We wanted to spend some time at the beach, and we wanted to spend a few days at the typical Disney attractions, but did not desire to do them all. We also wanted to try to get to the Kennedy Space Center. All of these activities were in central Florida, but ranged from one side of the state to the other. In order to accomplish all of this, we had to do some careful pre-planning. When we got there, there were two small glitches, but because we had planned ahead, we were able to manage those just fine and still accomplish our goals.

My family loves the outdoors, but if I do not plan a hike each week and watch the weather for the ideal day, we may never get around to doing it. We also love to do art projects. If I do not organize those supplies, make sure we have supplies, suggest appropriate projects and times for doing them, art will not be all that fun. What does your family enjoy that would benefit from some planning? What are your goals and those of the other members of your family? Make sure that these are incorporated into your daily routine as you seek out what to do each day.

Some children benefit from some additional support in areas of goal setting and planning, finishing projects or meeting goals, organizing their time, and reminders. I do not believe that such supports are in opposition to an unschooled life. I firmly believe that providing those supports in those instances when your child needs them is responding to your child according to your knowledge of him, and it assists him in learning about what interests him. Isn't that what a loving parent who is a facilitator, guide, accountability partner, coach, and mentor does?

I hope the above tips are helpful in how to fill those hours with meaning. You may have already gotten some ideas from the chapters on young children and children aged eight to twelve. The important thing is that you make the most of the time you have with your children. They will never be this age again. Character gained in childhood lasts a lifetime, knowledge gained in childhood may not. Make sure you are investing in the eternal.

Study Questions

1. In your prayer time with God, what has He said to you about your homeschool?

2. What idols do you have in your life that keep you enslaved to curriculum?

3. Is it hard for you to play with your children? Why or why not?

4. What does living a full life mean to you?

5. What does "making life sparkly" mean to you?

6. What does it mean to educate through relationship?

Chapter 8

Some Q & A

Q: How is education through relationship different from preparing an education based on a child's learning style, gifts, interests, and preferences?

A: The latter education is still parent directed, and those factors are often used to determine what curriculum to use, not necessarily what life experiences or real materials the child might learn from. That said, there *are* areas of interest that may be difficult to study from a biblical perspective without a curriculum. For example, human anatomy and physiology texts from the library often reflect a liberal worldview and only so much can be learned from a museum or video. Your best resource may be a human anatomy and physiology text designed for Christian homeschoolers.

There is no difference if the parent is using those factors to determine how best to collaborate with her child in those cases where working together is ideal. We must be careful not to abuse our knowledge of our children. Many people use the above-mentioned factors as though they are the silver bullet to finding what they think will be the perfect curriculum, and when their children still object to doing it, they wonder why. After all, they painstakingly filled in all the personality quizzes and tests, sifted through many catalogs, and spent hours deciding on that ideal set of materials. The problem is the parents never asked the children for their input. Why not give the child the catalog and ask him what he'd like to learn about this year?

Q: Aren't we supposed to be doing our best for God? This doesn't sound like we are doing our best.

A: What does it mean to do our best? The world might say that doing the best by our children is to make sure we give them the best opportunities, the best teachers, the best materials, the best education possible. Is that God's best? Is the world's measure the same as God's measure? Are we doing our best to cultivate a love for Him and not ourselves? Are we doing our best to instill knowledge of Him or men? Is the goal to impress God or to impress people?

Q: This sounds like it could get expensive. Am I supposed to buy or borrow a bunch of stuff that I think my kids might like and just leave it around for them to discover?

A: Well, that is one way you could do things. However, the idea is to do things *with* your children. You might try something like, "Hey, I saw this cool book at the library that I thought you guys might like. There was this _____ on page 150 that looked pretty interesting. Maybe we could do that together. What do you think?"

Or, "You were asking a lot of questions about the moon last night. Did you know that some of the brighter stars are actually planets? Some people have even made up stories about the stars." You could offer to tell some stories that you've read or heard and encourage your child to make up some herself.

Or, you could take your children on a walk through the woods or prairie and ask rhetorical questions about what you see. "I wonder what that growth is on that tree over there?" "Look at all these little tracks. I wonder who made them?" "Why does it smell like that?" Maybe they will catch your sense of wonder and investigate the wild, too.

Buying a bunch of books, videos, CDs, games, or whatever and leaving them on the table or in the living room as though Santa visits your house regularly is not enough. You don't need to spend your whole paycheck. Your goal is not to provide entertainment. Children often do not know the merit of something until you engage them, especially with books and games. You must be interesting and interested. You must engage them. You must make life sparkle.

Q: This sounds like all you do is have fun all the time. Life isn't about having fun. How do kids learn that life is rough?
A: Why shouldn't life be fun? Why shouldn't people make money doing something that they find fun and fulfilling? Sure, all of us experience hardship and tragedy at some point in our lives and our children often experience those things in the course of their lives, too. Their best friends move away or begin to exclude them from the group. The family dog dies. Grandma gets sick and is hospitalized. Dad loses his job. If your children don't experience any of these things, they will feel the pain through someone they know.

Doing service together often exposes them to the realities of life. When they visit a widow or bring a meal to a new mother, when they make Christmas boxes for Samaritan's Purse, when they bring new clothes and food to the neighbor whose basement flooded, or when they befriend the immigrant family down the street, they will experience all the ups and downs that life has to offer. Learning should not be among those things that are difficult and unpleasant for children. Learning should be joyous, wonderful, and anticipated with fervor and zest.

Chapter 9

Record-Keeping and Structure

I t is definitely more difficult to keep records about what you are doing with your children if you are following this more natural, unschooling, approach. You are not awarding grades or point scores. You do not have a list of completed assignments or completed curriculum. Keeping good records will require a bit more work on your part. There are several ways to do this.

Scrapbook/notebook

This is a great method for those who naturally like to do scrapbooking, taking pictures, keeping brochures, postcards, letters, and other paraphernalia, and who like to chronicle their lives by showing it in full color. Doing this requires more than just an artistic bent (you can do it even if you are not creatively inclined; it just won't look as fancy). It requires planning, organization, and time. You must remember to take pictures of everything you do and save those booklets and papers from everywhere. You must keep everything in order and in a safe place, note the dates, and set aside time each day or week to work on the scrapbook. While this method can seem like a lot of work, it can also be very rewarding and fun. It also lends itself well to involving your children as they take pictures and collect things to include. Scrapbooking your homeschool year can be a great way to build a family history, something that will last a lifetime. It is definitely worth investing in!

One year, I did this and it was very satisfying. I did not do anything fancy. In fact, each page was just construction paper with some pictures and notebook paper glued to it. I wrote the dates in and asked the kids to make comments about the pictures in the space on the notebook paper. I also only included field trips in this scrapbook, not everyday creations. Even though it is incredibly basic, it remains one of my favorite records of homeschooling because it brings back memories more than any other method I have tried.

Mostly, we have done notebooking because, for me, it is the easiest. Notebooking can be similar to scrapbooking in that it can include photos, brochures, and the like, but it often includes so much more. Our notebooks have included drawings and paintings, homemade books, mapwork and writing samples, flower pressings, lapbooks, and more. I like it because each child has their own, and I just put everything from each individual in their respective notebook. At the end of the year, I can bundle it up, label it as "2009" or whatever year, and store it. While this method requires less time and effort than scrapbooking, it is also less organized. Sometimes the contents lose their significance later without some additional notes or contextual information. It can seem like a stack of *work* papers, rather than a record of a family's best moments together. However, if your state requires you to keep records and show someone else, this may be an appropriate way to "show your work" without having to do too much work.

Journal

Keeping a journal is much like keeping a diary of what you have done each day. Nowadays, many people blog, which is basically the same thing as a journal, only it's online instead of hidden under your pillow, locked up tight. This is a great method if you are inclined to writing, rather than art, but it is still rather time consuming. You must remember to jot down some notes each day or at least a few days a week. From these notes, you can later put together a written summary of your year, if required.

Below is a sample entry for an entire week from a journal I kept for a few years off and on:

Summary for February 5–9, 2007
Well, the Lord is continuing to teach me patience and about what a good day is. Hawk has needed to work on obedience this week and this took precedence over lessons on some days. As I listen and spend less time planning while spending more time being, I find that some of their not so good habits are learned from my own imperfections. It really is true that we often need to work on ourselves first if we want to see change in others. One of these is learning that there is an appropriate time for doing everything. I sometimes choose to do things at inappropriate times and need to be better about organizing my own time in order to be a better example. Another of these is not wanting to put forth extra effort to do something that is messy, takes awhile to set up or get materials for, or that takes more than a day or two to finish. I need to be more aware of this, recognize that it is a generational habit, and consciously

work to be different so that they will learn to put forth the extra effort.

This was a week that did not feel very productive, but in fact, was quite productive. **Spanish** was consistent on most days and has been a great family activity. For **language arts**, Tiger read *Alice in Wonderland*, finished book 2 of *A Series of Unfortunate Events*, and wrote a short story with illustrations. She also wrote a few poems. I feel that I may need to provide more encouragement or more age appropriate copywork for this area so that some actual instruction takes place. There are many mechanical and spelling errors in her writing. I introduced ten new words to Hawk for his reading program and we reviewed the old words, but because of his disobedience, we did not get to do lessons as often as I would have liked. We did a lot of **math**. Tiger and I played Sum Swamp, and we played Place Value Toss and the Great Exchange with Hawk. Tiger and I reviewed her 2, 5, and 10 times tables and they read *From 1 to 100*. Hawk got lots of counting practice and I listened to him count to 20 (and even higher!) without a mistake. He has been trying hard to demonstrate that he knows how to count to 100. I think he understands the pattern but sometimes fumbles with the recitation. The U.S. Mint website was a popular place this week as Tiger used it to begin her France project that she decided to do, do a Lewis and Clark adventure game with Hawk, and try out some of their other games. For **history**, we read chapters 1–5 of *Theras and His Town* and did the accompanying activities from the study guide. Hawk drew some pictures of Greek objects/scenes as well. Tiger and Hawk also read their *God's World News* newspapers. **Science** activities included a visit to the Chicago Children's Museum, which had a special exhibit about sound waves. We spent a lot of time in that exhibit. I read two stories from *Among the Forest People*. Tiger had made a science lab in her room and gave me a lesson in human anatomy and how it compared with animals. She and Hawk started a bean-growing project and spent time with their kitchen chemistry set. Other things we did this week include reading the Bible together (Tiger finished *Letters to a Little Princess* book) and a playdate with friends. They listened to classical music, but not as much as previous weeks and they had their extracurricular classes (gym or swimming). They also made pretzels.

I must note that Butterfly and Mouse were not included in the above entry because Butterfly was two-and-a-half and Mouse wasn't born yet. There was an emphasis on noting activities that could be counted as *school*, and there were probably other things that we did that did not fit nicely into those educational categories. I knew that I would later have to go through my notes to create a summary of what we did all year, so I highlighted some words to help me reference activities later. Here is a chronicle of a single, recent day:

May 21, 2011

Today I woke up later than usual and was rather surprised that Mouse and Butterfly had not come down to wake me up. Ed and I sat talking for awhile and then we went upstairs for breakfast. Mouse and Butterfly had been playing in the front room and had brought a bunch of stuffed animals in there. Butterfly said they were in school. Tiger came down soon after we did and about an hour later, Hawk came down. We had decided that we were going to go to the Civil War reenactment at Naper Settlement today and investigated the timing of the events and how to get there. After we had showered, we were off. It was supposed to rain today, but of course, it did not rain and turned out to be a beautiful day! I got some great pictures of Hawk as a part of the recruitment of soldiers, the staged battle, the medicine show, and Abraham Lincoln. We didn't know that the battles were so loud. Tiger and Butterfly seemed most impressed with the field hospital. Mouse was just as interested in the battle as Hawk and had to pretend with the other boys after it was over. When we returned, the boys and Ed played Nerf gun skirmishes in the kitchen while I made dinner and then Tiger and I went to a performance put on by kids in Circle Urban Ministries. The kids did a great job. After the little ones were in bed, I worked on the computer and Ed and Hawk talked about nuclear fusion and bombs. Hawk has been very interested in nuclear energy after watching a Tales of the Dead show on PBS about nuclear bombs. Then we went to bed. What a full day.

Like a scrapbook, you can see that journaling or blogging can be a chronicle of your life together as a family, but it is much more cumbersome to create a report of the school year from a journal than from a scrapbook. If you do not feel particularly creative or feel the process of shooting, developing, and organizing photos is more cumbersome than just writing, perhaps keeping a journal of your year will be the best record-keeping tool for you.

Portfolio

A portfolio is a collection of your child's best work. It can be a combination of different items. For example, let's say your daughter spent a lot of time one month reading biographical books about the Holocaust, you visited the Peace Museum in Skokie, Illinois, and your daughter decided to write a story about a fictitious survivor of a concentration camp. You might include in her portfolio the following: a list of the books she read, a brochure from the museum with photos of her on the premises, and most of all, a typed copy of her fictional account of this historical atrocity. Let's say the next month, she creates a small museum out of her collection of tree leaves and seeds, mounting each item in small cases and frames. You might encourage her to have a neighborhood showing of her collection and give a short talk to the kids about each of the items. You would then include in her portfolio several photos of her displays, a transcript of her talk, and if she distributed flyers, a copy of one of those as well. As you can see, a portfolio both tells and shows what your child has done. It is a bit like a scrapbook, but is more personal to each child than a scrapbook would normally be. This is also the style of record keeping most helpful to a teen trying to show his competence to potential employers and colleges, as we discussed a little bit in the last chapter. It is what professionals use.

Other Alternatives
1. Keep reading lists.
2. Develop a family webpage.
3. *Simply Charlotte Mason* website has an easy-to-use system to keep track of what you are reading and doing. It also allows you to print reports. There is a fee associated with this.
4. There are several computer-based homeschool record-keeping systems available, such as ***www.homeschooltracker.com*** or ***www.homeschoolsolutions.com***.

I have no affiliation with any of these companies and do not endorse one over another. I am simply mentioning them for your convenience and benefit.

Whatever record-keeping system you choose, make sure that you are satisfied with it and you are in accordance with the laws of your state. Some state laws are more difficult to comply with than others

when it comes to a natural style of learning. If you have questions about the laws in your state, you can go to the Homeschool Legal Defense Association website and look them up, ask other unschoolers in your state, or find your laws on the Home Education magazine website listed in the Resources section of this book.

The Importance of Being Organized

Of course, it will be difficult to implement any record keeping if you do not have an organization strategy. This will affect not just your system of tracking your homeschool year, but also your home environment and the flow of your days. Natural learning is about choice; it is not about chaos. Having a routine does not undermine having choices. Children need a predictable routine in order to navigate their lives, and just because they might choose what they'd like to learn doesn't mean that they don't need any daily structure to help them organize their time or their belongings.

Have you ever walked into a well-organized home and felt yourself suddenly relax? If you and your children are constantly searching for the paintbrushes, the new book about Japanese culture that you couldn't wait to read, the baseball schedule, or matching shoes, you are probably all too familiar with the feelings of frustration and chaos. Organization just makes living easier. There are lots of great books and online resources for cleaning and organizing your spaces. One of the most popular is Fly Lady (www.flylady.net). The most important thing is to get started. Start with one room. Have three bins: to give away, to throw away, and to keep. This can be a teaching opportunity for the kids, too, about more than just having a place for everything. Frugality, helping others, gratitude, and more come to mind. When you are all done, you can celebrate your accomplishment together.

Dr. Adam Cox, a clinical psychologist who speaks nationally about executive function skills, writes in his book *No Mind Left Behind* that organization and planning are two of the essential brain skills needed for success. Planning and organization are the management of time and space, not learning. Effective planning is characterized by thinking ahead, defining a sequence of steps in order to reach a goal, and time awareness. Effective organization makes us feel calmer, enhances feelings of control, and of being effective. Organization also propels productivity.

Planning and Predictable Routine

Part of effective planning is having a predictable routine. It helps children develop flexible thinking. Cox writes, "It is easier for a child to learn to be flexible and to be less anxious during changes and transitions if there is a regular schedule or routine." Children need predictability in order to feel safe and that their needs will be met. If a child never knows when he is going to be leaving the house, for example, he might never feel comfortable allowing himself to become completely immersed in a play activity for fear he will be interrupted at any time. If a child never knows when lunch might be, he might be prone to snacking all day (although there are plenty of children who snack all day regardless). An unpredictable life actually stresses a child unnecessarily because she has to constantly be thinking about things that, if there were predictability, would be a habitual routine requiring no thought at all.

This principle became especially important to Butterfly and Mouse. Butterfly still asks for a list of what she needs to do each day, even though she chose all the activities and subjects. She becomes anxious if there is no written plan and has been known to spend blocks of time flipping through catalogs and magazines instead of doing productive work. Mouse likes to know *the day before* whether or not we are going someplace. He insists on this, even if it is a place he goes every week and that he greatly enjoys, such as parkour or the library homeschool meet-up. He growls and threatens if he doesn't get that warning.

Charlotte Mason says that making decisions is the most difficult thing a person has to do and a child should not be burdened with this.

The formation of good habits through routines helps eliminate the burden of decision making for basic life needs. She talked a lot about the importance of habit formation in young children. She says that the only means a teacher may use to educate children are the child's natural environment, *the training of good habits*, and exposure to living ideas and concepts. She expands on her motto of "Education is an atmosphere, a discipline, a life," particularly the discipline aspect, by saying that we train a child to have good habits and self-control. She takes great pains in *Home Education* to outline exactly what mothers should do to train their children in good habits of body, mind, and spirit. If you are interested in her ideas, you can find a wonderful book, *Laying Down the Rails*, at www.simplycharlottemason.com.

Planning can help your family accomplish goals. Grace Llewellyn, director of Not Back to School Camp and author, writes in *Teenage Liberation Handbook* "In a mostly 'unstructured education, you let life happen to you, keeping your eyes open and learning from whatever you happen to do. In a mostly 'structured' education, you make life happen, setting goals and making plans... don't assume that structure has to be *school*-style structure." Having blocks of time in the day for certain activities, such as Chores, Bible Time, Exercise, Table Time, Project Time, Read-Aloud Time, or however you spend your time, is helpful. The key is to alternate active and passive times and to assess how you want to be spending your time and what are the ways that your children naturally spend their time.

It is also important to thoughtfully consider how you would like your children to be spending their free time. Do you want your children spending two hours a day in front of a screen? Do you want your children spending several hours a day listening to rock music on their headphones or reading fantasy novels? If you do not want these things in your home, then you will have to provide guidance toward what you feel is acceptable. This may mean purchasing additional craft supplies or building materials or other needed items. Young children also need help with setting goals and attaining those goals. Without us as guides, they will have a difficult time with this skill. However, the goals need to be *their* goals and they need to be the ones deciding what are the best ways to reach those goals, even if we are guiding them in how to break down those goals into incremental tasks.

The key is to keep it simple and manageable. Here are some great tips that have been extremely helpful to me: get up before the children, get your home and life organized, do chores in the morning, have a regular meal-planning day, do all your errands on one day, have a family read-aloud time, a "table" time, and assess yours and your children's free time activities. You need to decide what will work for you based on your lifestyle and needs, but know that unschooling does not mean unglued. Unschooling simply means freedom to choose learning activities. Please feel free to put routines in place. You and your children need them, even if you change them from time to time.

Study Questions

1. Which record-keeping method most appeals to you?

2. What changes will you need to make to your current record-keeping strategy in order to make it more unschool-friendly?

3. What do the laws in your state require and how will this impact how you record your unschooling lifestyle?

Concluding Remarks

I hope you have been challenged by the concepts presented in this book. We discussed what the Bible says about educating children and discovered that the world's way of doing things doesn't really line up with God's way. We need to respect how God created each child. We need to seek Him and trust Him with our children. We learned about the best ways to motivate our children and how the practices of punishments and rewards in order to coerce and control children is unbiblical. We uncovered better ways to interact with them.

We took a deep dive into each developmental stage and found that, at each point, our culture doesn't get it right. We need to do things differently, even if we are criticized for it. Our little children need lots of free play and sunshine. Our older children need opportunities to try new things and succeed, including service and entrepreneurship. Our teens need to take the helm of their lives and do hard things. Through it all, we need to look for what God is doing in their hearts so we can participate with Him and not be a hindrance.

We also found that we benefit from structure and organization, even as we lead a different sort of life with our children.

I encourage you to continue to seek the Lord while you transform your relationships with your children. God bless you and your homeschooling journey!

About the Author

 Julie Polanco started walking in the love and grace of Jesus Christ in 2000. She is active in the women's ministry and on the worship team at a nondenominational evangelical church in the Chicago area. She and her husband have homeschooled their four children from the beginning, graduating their first in 2016. Julie is a regular contributor for *Old Schoolhouse Magazine* and their Homeschooling with Heart blog and is the high school botany instructor for www.schoolhouseteachers.com.

Her involvement in the homeschool community includes serving on the board of her local support group, starting her own support group, and teaching science and writing classes in her home and in cooperatives. Currently, she maintains a blog that discusses homeschooling, Christian living, and the writing life at www.juliepolancobooks.com

In addition to being active in her church, the homeschool community, and continuing to teach her children, Julie is a professional freelance writer. Her work appears in health and wellness, food, and trade publications. She also ghostwrites books for others.

Visit her website:
www.juliepolancobooks.com

Get additional resources, including
50 Ways to Motivate Your Child,
by signing up at the website.

Find resources, sample transcripts, and other helpful information. Follow Julie on Facebook @juliepolancobooks.

If you have been blessed by this book, help others by leaving a review on your favorite bookstore's website. Thanks!

Bibliography

Albert, David. *Just Do the Math.* Have fun. Learn stuff. Grow. Common Courage Press, Maine. 2006.

Boles, Blake. College Without High School. New Society Publishers, Canada. 2009.

Brown, Dr. Stuart. Play: How it Shapes the Brain, Opens the Imagination, and Invigorates the Soul. Penguin Group, New York. 2009.

Cox, Dr. Adam. No Mind Left Behind: Understanding and Fostering Executive Control—The Eight Essential Brain Skills Every Child Needs to Thrive. Penguin Group, New York. 2007.

Davis, Chris and Ellen. I Saw the Angel in the Marble. Elijah Press, Tennessee. 2004.

DeMille, Oliver Van. A Thomas Jefferson Education. George Wythe College Press, Utah. 2006.

Elkind, Dr. David. Miseducation: Preschoolers at Risk. Knopf, 1987.

Field, Christina. Life Skills for Kids: Equipping Your Child for the Real World. WaterBrook Press, Colorado. 2000.

Gatto, John Taylor. Guerilla Education Seminar at In Home Homeschooling Conference, March 2010.

Gray, Peter. www.psychologytoday.com/blog/freedom-learn. February 24, 2010. April 15, 2010.

Hannaford, Carla. Smart Moves: Why Learning is Not All in Your Head. Great Ocean Publishers, 1995.

Healy, Dr. Jane. Endangered Minds. Simon and Schuster, New York. 1990.

Holt, John. Learning All the Time. DaCapo Press, 1989.

Holt, John and Farenga, Patrick. Teach Your Own: The John Holt Book of Homeschooling. DaCapo Press, 2003.

Hood, Dr. Mary. The Relaxed Home School. Ambleside Educational Press, Maryland. 1994.

Kohn, Alfie. Punished by Rewards. Houghton Mifflin, New York. 1993.

Lavoie, Richard. The Motivational Breakthrough. Simon and Schuster, New York. 2007.

Levy, Nathan. Parent Seminar. Worlds of Wisdom and Wonder, LaGrange, IL. Summer 2006.

Llewellyn, Grace. The Teenage Liberation Handbook. Lowry House Publishers, Oregon. 1998.

Lockhart, Paul. A Mathematician's Lament. 2002. reprinted here: www.maa.org/devlin/devlin_03_08.html

Louv, Richard. Last Child in the Woods: Saving Our Children from Nature-Deficit Disorder. Algonquin Books of Chapel Hill, North Carolina. 2005.

Mason, Charlotte. Paraphrase by Leslie Noelani Laurio. Toward a Philosophy of Education. www.lulu.com. 2005.

Mercogliano, Chris. In Defense of Childhood. Beacon Press, Boston. 2007.

Moore, Dr. Raymond and Dorothy. The Successful Homeschool Family Handbook. Thomas Nelson, Inc., Tennessee. 1994.

Moore, Dr. Raymond and Dorothy. Better Late Than Early. Reader's Digest Press, Washington. 1975.

Ratey, Dr. John. Spark: The Revolutionary New Science of Exercise and the Brain. Little, Brown, and Co., 2008.

Tyler, Zan. 7 Tools for Cultivating Your Child's Potential. B & H Publishing Group, Tennessee. 2005.

Morgan James
Speakers Group

www.TheMorganJamesSpeakersGroup.com

We connect Morgan James published
authors with live and online events
and audiences who will benefit
from their expertise.

 Morgan James makes all of our titles available
through the Library for All Charity Organization.

www.LibraryForAll.org

Printed in the USA
CPSIA information can be obtained
at www.ICGtesting.com
JSHW082337140824
68134JS00020B/1724